Discovered

2013 Poetry Collection

Discovered represents our student authors as accurately as possible.
Every effort has been made to print each poem
as it was submitted with minimal editing
of spelling, grammar, and punctuation.
All submissions have been formatted to this compilation.

Published by
The America Library of Poetry
P.O. Box 978
Houlton, ME 04730
Website: www.libraryofpoetry.com
Email: generalinquiries@libraryofpoetry.com

Printed in the United States of America.

THE AMERICA
LIBRARY OF POETRY

ISBN: 978-0-9773662-8-6

Contents

Poetry by Division

Discovered

In memory of two of our student authors
Arione' A. Fulton and Kellie Ann Sharp

The Story of My Eyes
by Arione' A. Fulton (1999 – February 10, 2013)

I'm known for being cold-hearted and mean
But when you look beyond my eyes you'll see my story
I was the girl who loved and laughed at everything
Now when you look at me you see nothing
I could tell you myself but what difference would it make
My pretty little heart will forever break
When I think about what my story was
This is exactly what it does
Leaves me sitting there
With the pain, I just can't seem to bear
My story will be forever hidden
But not to the people who hold the secrets I have given

Girl In the Mirror
by Kellie Ann Sharp (1996 – August 23, 2013)

Every day I look in the mirror, every day I see the same thing.
This sad looking girl, someone broken inside.
Her eyes reveal the pain she's endured,
her smile hardly existent, most of the time fake.
She looks so sad, why? Why is she sad?
Nobody knows except the girl in the mirror.
Nobody knows of the broken family she comes from.
Nobody knows she's been used and abused.
Nobody knows that at 15 she's experienced the loss of a child.
Nobody knows she battles with herself every day.
Nobody can see that for her, living to the next day is her biggest goal.
Nobody knows. Why? She keeps it to herself.
She feels the world just wants to hurt her. She's been hurt by many.
She doesn't trust any. It's her against the world. She fights this battle by herself.
So many people have walked out on her so she's used to being alone.
She's tired of people leaving so she keeps a distance.
Never getting close to anyone to feel anything.
The girl in the mirror just wants to scream.
She wants to be heard but no one will listen. She fears her past will happen again.
She fears of trusting the wrong people. She fears losing those she loves.
She fears getting hurt again. I guess you could say she fears living.
That girl in the mirror wants to be free. That girl in the mirror is me.

Foreword

There are two kinds of writers in the world.
There are those who write from experience,
and those who write from imagination.
The experienced, offer words that are a reflection of their lives.
The triumphs they have enjoyed, the heartaches they have endured;
all the things that have made them who they are,
they graciously share with us, as a way of sharing themselves,
and in doing so, give us, as readers, someone to whom we may relate,
as well as fresh new perspectives
on what may be our common circumstances in life.
From the imaginative,
come all the wonderful things we have yet to experience;
from sights unseen, to sounds unheard.
They encourage us to explore the limitless possibilities
of our dreams and fantasies,
and aid us in escaping, if only temporarily,
the confines of reality and the rules of society.
To each, we owe a debt of gratitude;
and rightfully so, as each provides a service of equal importance.
Yet, without the other, neither can be truly beneficial.
For instance, one may succeed in accumulating a lifetime of experience,
only to consider it all to have been predictable and unfulfilling,
if denied the chance to chase a dream or two along the way.
Just as those whose imaginations run away with them never to return,
may find that without solid footing in the real world,
life in fantasyland is empty.
As you now embark, dear reader,
upon your journey through these words to remember,
you are about to be treated to both heartfelt tales of experience,
and captivating adventures of imagination.
It is our pleasure to present them for your enjoyment.
To our many authors,
who so proudly represent the two kinds of writers in the world,
we dedicate this book, and offer our sincere thanks;
for now, possibly more than ever,
the world needs you both.

Paul Wilson Charles
Editor

Editor's Choice Award

The Editor's Choice Award is presented
to an author who demonstrates not only
the solid fundamentals of creative writing,
but also the ability to elicit an emotional response
or provide a thought provoking body of work
in a manner which is both clear and concise.

You will find "The Beholder"
by Bri Lewis on page 145 of *Discovered*

2013
Spirit of Education
For Outstanding Participation

Blakeney
Elementary School

Waynesboro,
Georgia

Presented to participating students and faculty
in recognition of your commitment
to literary excellence.

Division I

*Grades
3-5*

Pride In America
by Kaylee Freitas

The American Flag has 50 stars.
Just like Mars, it burns bright red.
The American Flag has 13 stripes.
Flies like a kite so wild and free.
The American Flag's colors are Red, White, and Blue.
The Flag was made for me and you.

Spring Is Finally Here
by Kennedy Ellis

Spring is right here
The birds are back and singing with joy
The flowers have grown
And the leaves on the trees are here
And now the children can play at the park
And the rabbits are hopping
And so now you know that
Spring is a wonderful thing

A Simple Man
by Makayla Nnaji

I saw a man sitting on my porch.
I had never seen that man before.
Then I asked my mom who was that man.
She said that he was a good man.
A outdoor man who liked to go fishing, swimming, and play basketball.
What he most liked to do was greet new people.
My mother told me that he was a simple man who had always been around
I just never noticed him.
When he saw there was a new person on the street
he would say hi and ask them if they needed any help.
Then I just remembered that my mom was supposed
to take me to see someone I have not seen in years.
Then when me and my mom got over to their house I knew that smile.
My mom said, do you recognize him? I said yes but I forgot his name.
She said are you ready for me to tell you who it is.
I said yes. She said, it's your father. I was so surprised to see him.
I gave him a hug and said I love you.

Volcanoes
by Jordan Richmond

Volcanoes
Glowing, Red
Brown, Erupting, Molten lava
A cone shaped hill or mountain.
A volcano

Mirror
by Heather Ward

As I look in the mirror,
I hope to see my dreams reflecting back at me.
But that wasn't to be.
All I can see is me.

School
by Kira Koeller

Education, education
Good job, good job
I am going to college
To be an artist
Yay for me, yay for me
No hobo, no hobo
Mat is good, algebra too
Could you be a teacher?
Could you be a sculptor?
Yay for me, yay for me
Still in school, still in school
4th grade, 5th grade
We can all do it
It is fun
Good for you, good for you
Diploma, diploma
We did it, we did it
We are done with school
Until next year
In college, in college

Sight
by Matthew Artuso

ERIE purple
reveals to different shades of pink,
as the ever changing colors of the roof
of the world casts long shadows.
They dart through the sky, creating
quick shadows on the ground, as flying squirrels glide to see
the last of the orange and yellow sight in the sky.
Whoosh, Whoosh. Rolling, Bashing
rolls of Blue and White
crashing on the cliff side,
like the thump of a heart on every beat.
A lively but relaxing chirping
comes from the bundle of greens and dirt.
Dense, hot air brushes up in queue
with the rolling shades of
white and blue,
Look out and see the
beautiful crested sky brushes up on the waves,
What a Sight!

January
by Payton MacKinnon

January, winter, so many words to describe such a lonely time of the year.
Trees shed their leaves so they look stone cold and bony.
An icy chill fills the atmosphere like a bottle of nitrogen exploded everywhere.
I feel lonely, no animals to comfort me.
I feel like a bug, trapped in a spider web of shame.
Why can't I be happy?
Because of the cold?
No. I feel like a piece of happiness was ripped out of me.
And the only way to rebuild that happiness is spring.
All of this could be here.
The only thing stopping it is January.
A road block in the circle of life.
Disallowing the fog to disappear.
Or the beautiful pines to get their colorful friends back.
All of this could be here.
Except there is one problem ... January.

My Poem
by Amelia Kochany

Here's my poem:
here it goes,
1, 2, 3, 4, watch a movie or do more
like sing or dance
sing and dance.
It's so much fun.
They are!

Nature
by JJ Hook

The tree is small, old, peeling, and crunching.
It smells like maple.
The air is good.
I can hear the leaves crunching under my feet.
The leaves on the ground feel like an old man's hands.
I can see the black and orange birds.
The white bugs look like a fairy.
When I hold the rocks in my hand, it feels rough and hard.
The trees look very old and rough.

Ms. Gwichen
by Lamar Lee

Ms. Gwichen was sitting in her kitchen
Eating some chicken
She found it on the ground yesterday
The chicken was old and it had mold
But Ms. Gwichen hasn't ate in 5 days.
So she picked up the chicken
And ate it to the bone
Then it made her fall asleep.
From her head to her feet
She was sick with a cold.
When she woke up
She started to quack like a duck.
The chicken put her in a trance
That made her get up and dance
to the bathroom when she made herself put on some cream
That's the last thing she remembered until she woke up from this crazy dream.

American Flag
by Kaeden Woodworth

It has 50 stars
I'm playing on the monkey bars.
It has 13 stripes
I'm out flying kites
It has 3 colors of Red, White, and Blue
The flag gives you freedom
As it was made for me and you

Jupiter
by Cole Crabtree

Jupiter
Jupiter
Big, red spot
It's not suitable for humans
There might be aliens
It's so big
It's so big
Jupiter Jupiter
Aliens aliens
If it had them, they would be purple
It's so big
It's so big

A Sight To Behold
by Elijah Johnson

It flows like calm silent water
It's vivid green and yellow calms your beating heart
When the sun touches, it takes your breath and replaces it with the warmth
The swift rabbit dashes across to get some flowers.
When you look at it you can feel it pulling you
Its softness molds to your feet embracing it
The bees hum as they gracefully float across its vast expanse
At dawn the bright and cool pinks, purples, reds,
and oranges come out to play.
Created by one Man who formed each delicate flower
and grass piece by hand with His care and love
This Man is God who created this beautiful meadow.

Gardening With My Papa
by Phil Bell

My papa and I went into his garden. It was really cool.
There were carrots and cauliflower.
It was really cool. Then we started to eat them.
My dog came running out and wrecked everything.
That is now his name ... Wrecker

Nature Is ...
by Sean Henigan

Nature is green
Nature is blue
Nature is everywhere
Nature does everything for me and you.
Nature is the greatest.
Nature is the deepest.
Nature is wild.
Nature is beauty.
Nature is the World.
Nature can be moody.
It's seasons can give you a fright,
But don't worry, nature is a beautiful sight.

A Tribute To My Uncle Chelone Miller
by Iris Miller-White

Sensing the world around him
Feeling his surroundings
Trusting nature and Mother Earth
Accepting the world and its people
Changing the world around him
Flying off the jump like a bird
Different since the accident
He changed since that day
He valued every second
He savored every minute
If he could sense the world around him
Could he have known what was going to happen?
If he did, why didn't he call to say good-bye?
Why didn't he tell us he was going to die?

My Dog Pandora
by Molly Massey

I got Pandora 4 years ago.
Pandora barks at strangers to keep us safe.
Pandora licks us head to toe.
Pandora plays in the mud.
Pandora acts super funny.
Pandora sometimes chews up my stuff.
But Pandora says "ruff!" to tell me she's sorry.
I love my Rottweiler Pandora.
And it will always stay that way.

Autumn
by Jing Yi Lovick

In autumn,
The wind whistles through the trees
Her leaves dance free
Caught by the grass.
One, another, each a different color.
Red orange, yellow, brown and sometimes green.
Each dry leaf wrinkles up,
Exploding in a crunchy sound!
It mixes in the ground,
no longer a leaf you see.

Santa's Elves
by Heidi Kirschner

Pound, pound, tap, tap, tap
The elves are making toys
Yellow, purple, pink, and green
All sorts of colors that are seen
Wrapping paper, ribbons, and more
Oh my gosh, it's elves galore
Stamp, stamp, stamp
The elves are on a rampage
Squealing and laughter fill the air
Christmas joy is already here
Santa Claus is coming here
And his elves are also drawing near
To visit us on Christmas night
And hopefully you'll catch a sight.

Christmas Is So Fun
by Fabian Chartier

Sometimes we run
The snow is falling
One by one we hope it will be gone

Nightmare
by Micaela Stanton

Ghosts and ghouls are frightening
But watch out for the lightning
It will give you a shock,
To send you down the block
Watch as a full moon grows
Will werewolves come out, who knows?
Eating meat is what they do
So you'd better hide or they'll find you
You think candy is so sweet
I want a tasty treat
But watch out, bats will eat it all
Right here at the Halloween ball
The night is over, goodbye
Shake my hand, don't be shy
Suddenly I wake up in my bed
And realize it's just in my head

Life
by Jordan Saylor

There's nothing better than your family or friends
Or what your career will be like when it ends,
But beware, life goes by fast
So make sure you make it last.
Some people might want to be singers, magicians, teachers or musicians,
And those will be your life making decisions.
If you just believe
Then no one will grieve.
Don't grieve, don't leave,
Don't cry, don't lie, don't say goodbye.
Remember this, there's nothing more important than your family or friends.
But when the time is right I want to say the end.

The Day
by Brielyn Lisowski

My life is so boring
Night and day
So every morning
I jump in a pile of hay
Although it is not fun
'Cuz my birthday is in May
I now jump in the Bay

Blue
by Lauren Tremper

Blue is the sky that is right above us.
Blue is the water that is all over the Earth.
Blue as the color of the ocean's eyes.
Blue as the ocean's breeze that comes to your face.
Blue can be a sad thing.
Blue can be the color of a baby's tear.
Blue can be the color of the old rocking chair.
Blue as the color of a pretty girl's headband.
Blue makes me a nice person.
Blue is one of the colors I like.

Dreams
by Brendan VanderMeer

Dreams are something you strive for.
You can't just stop when something gets in your way.
You can't take no for an answer.
If you do, your life won't be the way you want it to be
Do you think Michael Jordan gave up his dream just
'cause he didn't make the high school basketball team?
Well no he didn't.
He practiced so much because you know what he did to him.
It made him perfect at basketball.
That's why he is so good at basketball
So believe in yourself.
Follow your passion
Follow what you're good at
Follow your dreams
And some day it may just come true.

My Big Dream
by Olivia Schneider

My big dream
Would be to see
A world of pure imagination
and to see everyone get along
to see a world of peace and love
To have no wars, To have no fights
With a smile on everyone's face
That's my big, big dream

Do You Dream
by Rylei Roseberry

Do you dream about being a spy
and crawling through laser beams?
Do you ever dream about walking on a cloud
and then shout "come to me birds" out loud?
Do you dream?
Well do you dream?
Do you dream like me?
Well I have some big big dreams so ...
I hope you don't dream like me

Friendship Is Freedom
by Logan Hinson

Friendship is freedom.
It is courage and understanding.
Friendship is help.
It is getting to know someone.
Friendship is fun.
It is time to share.
Friendship is freedom with one another.
It is cherishing God's word.
Friendship is prayer and love.
It is time to get along.
Friendship is peace on Earth.
It is clean up.
Friendship is freedom.

It
by Ayla Wood

You get it at school,
Kids do not like to get it,
Teachers give us it.
(Homework)

Flowers
by Rachael Velmer

Flowers
Pretty colorful
Smelling, blossoming, growing
Roses, lilies, daffodil, bleeding hearts
Attracting, leafing, blooming
Thorny nectar
Blossoms

Rollover Rover
by Grant Malek

One day there was a pet Rover,
who didn't know how to roll over.
So the owner said, "Just try,
or you may die!"
Rover, Rover, please roll over!
But he didn't.
So that made the owner really sad
and mad!
The next day the owner said, "Rover, roll over!"
But it was night,
so Rover took a huge bite.
The next day,
he went to the bay.
Rover, please lay down!
But Rover ran to town!
I will make
and bake
treats for Rover.
He took a treat,
that was not neat.
In town he was down.

Blue
by Danielle Talpesh

Blue is the color of the waves washing upon the shore.
Blue is the color of the sky so clear.
Blue reminds me of surfing on the clear blue waves.
Blue is as fancy as a pretty blue dress.
Blue is the color of the water I swim in every day.
Blue is the color of dolphins that live in the deep blue sea.
Blue is my most favorite color of all.

Snowflake
by Deanna Delliss

The life of a snowflake is wonderful
I'll fall but always land in snow
Always I'll know
I never started out as snow
All my life
I have tried to see
Through my millions of brothers and sisters
To the life I once knew
When I know I will never be with you

Christmas
by Margaret Willette

Christmas is a holiday,
A very special day.
That Jesus Christ was born,
On that very Christmas morn.
We have a Christmas tradition,
That it is no competition,
To be the first to open presents
At those very special moments.
Santa comes down the chimney,
To give presents to you and me.
He pulls them out of his bag,
For let's not brag.
He goes to every house that night,
Even before it gets light.
But Christmas has a different meaning,
Than just the little beginning.

Blue
by Alexis Peters

Blue is for the ocean
Where the fish splash
Blue is when the rain pours down
Blue far beyond the ocean seas
Lies the secret kept for me
Blue was when the seas were flooded
Blue is graceful like the waves
Blue is more than just a color

High
by Ehab Mozeb

Higher than the twin towers that got demolished on 9/11
Higher than the Leaning Tower of Pisa
Higher than Davison's Meap scores
Higher than a T-rex eating a cave man
Higher than the tallest skyscraper
Higher than the circle shaped moon
Higher than a furry giant
Higher than a rocket ship landing on Mars
Higher than Mount Everest, the tallest mountain
Higher than the Statue of Liberty in New York
That's how high I really want to fly!

Happy
by Mohammad Muhaimin

Happier than a bird of paradise singing on a branch
Happier than getting a new muscle car and driving happily ever after
Happier than adopting a puppy that is wagging its tail
Happier than getting a trophy in a Big Monster Truck Jam
Happier than getting good presents on Christmas
Happier than getting good grades in school
Happier than being a lawyer and fighting for justice
Happier than being famous in Hollywood, California
Happier than being a President of your country
Happier than being a NASA astronaut and blasting to Mars
That's how happy you could be as a millionaire

Black
by Blake Davis

Black is the color of the sky at night.
Black is the color of the smoke of a fire.
Black is the color of the stripes on a zebra's back.
Black is the color of the pupil in my eye.
Black is the color of the tires on a car.
Black is the color of the tiles on a roof.
Black is the color of my pants.
Black is the color of the seats of my car.
Black is the color of sin in the world.
Black is the color of the darkness in my heart.

My Dancing Pens
by Aarohi Darisi

My crazy, dazzling dancing pens work all day long.
Whatever they do is absolutely never wrong.
They burst out vibrant colors that are eye-catching and strong.
They cheerfully dance around singing a melodious song.
The beautiful colors flow out like a waterfall,
They can draw anything from a circle to the Taj Mahal.
Reds, yellows, blues, purples and greens
Jump on the paper like jumping beans.
The results are always detailed and beautiful,
Well of course! It's a rainbow that is super colorful.
I am thankful to have color filling this world,
and decorating our environment filled with swirl!

Greek gods
by Jordan Robichaud

Some people believe in Greek gods
But I think their powers are very superior and odd.
There were brothers called the big three,
They were very strong and powerful, unlike me.
They were feared most of all, for they made all but one Titan fall.
But not all Titans did die.
Like Kronos, for his powers were feared on high.
So the Titan war had begun.
But Kronos lost, and the gods won.
And some believe the gods didn't die,
Because their powers were feared on high.

Time
by Elizabeth Ballmann

The sun goes up, the sun goes down
The seasons change, the years go 'round
But in all that time you see,
I never forget what matters to me.

Vine Snake
by Axl Clay

Snake
Green, brown
Hanging, looking, eating
It is very still
Vine snake

The Question
by Decklyn Leahy

We were at the zoo,
I asked you the question,
You said I do,
Me and you together,
Best friends forever,
I love you.

Mama's Prayer
by Chelsea Potvin

I asked God what I'm feeling
I couldn't identify, my footsteps were light
my thoughts were bright
I felt as I could fly
I laughed and though I was happy, I let out a gentle sigh.
I knew one day she would be gone
and I'd have her no more
but until that day shows its face upon me
I will ignore DEATH'S door.

The Sun & Moon
by Viola Dengler

The sun is hot
The sun is red
The sun comes up from the East then sets at the West
But don't forget the stars come too
With the moon
The moon is white
The sky is dark blue
The moon comes up from the East then sets at the West
That's why the Sun and Moon are mostly alike

I Believe
by Brooke Beyer

One day I looked outside and couldn't believe my eyes,
I saw a man in a robe or cloak with a ring above His head,
I hurry down the stairs and stumble to get a peek,
I tripped and fell onto the ground right below His feet,
"I can't believe my eyes!" I said looking at the piercings on His feet,
"Believe, my child," He said, "for I am Jesus Christ."

The Knight and the Soldier
by Andrea Vegliante

There once was a knight that proudly rode on his horse
There is a soldier who rides his dusty jeep with mighty force
From the knight his enemy began to run
Just as the solider began to chase his rival, and pulls out his gun
The knight's enemy stops and stands so fierce
As the soldier halts and his enemy stops
and the soldier's eyes are so focused they pierce
The knight pulls out his sword and begins to fight
Then the soldier aims his gun at his rival and then his face turns white
They both end it all as their rivals go down
The knight and the soldier both save a little town
Knights and soldiers aren't the same
Both brave and great that's how they came

Spring
by Bradey Anderson

Wet heavy raindrops
Snow banks disappearing fast
Branches falling

Meet My Snowman
by Kade Robillard

This is Mr. Snowman.
He's as white as a marshmallow,
his buttons black like coal,
fat as a hippo, hard like an icicle,
as tall as a skyscraper,
his scarf is soft as a kitten,
as fun as me.

Life As We Know It
by McKenzie McPhee-Frechette

I'm a loving kid with higher dreams,
Doing everything possible to make life as simple as it seems.
Never a day can go by when we aren't living life as if it were the last,
Never regretting things done in the past.
Life is only over when you think you have nothing left to do,
But sometimes I just keep living 'cause of you.
You're my inspiration to keep on living,
Just because of the love you keep on giving.
When we say our last words with our last breath,
Don't be scared because it's just death.
We'll be together in the after-years,
So let there be no tears,
And get rid of our fears.
Today is life as we know it,
And tomorrow we may have nothing to show for it.
But one thing is for sure,
Every day I wake up,
I love you more and more

Halloween Is Cool
by Izaac Lauscher

I don't want to boast
But I'm not afraid of a ghost
If you see a witch
Head for a ditch
I saw a bat
He tried to land on my hat
I told him to scat
That dirty flying rat
When I went to school
I thought I saw a ghoul
But there was nothing there fool
Halloween is so cool

Adventure
by Abigail Thomas

Have you ever wanted to run a race?
Travel around the world with grace?
Have an adventure that's out of sight?
It is quite a bit long of a flight.
You could travel through the air so free.
And see as far as the eye can see.
Now let's travel to the Americas, okay lad.
When you come here you won't be sad.
After let's travel to Europe, aye mates?
We'll catch a whale with our humongous baits.
Then we will travel to Africa and celebrate
Kwanzaa for 7 days straight.
Do you think we're done? Oh no!
We still have to travel to Asia. Let's go!
That was cool, we just went to Mongolia.
But now we need to proceed onward to Australia.
Let's travel to the North and South Pole.
Look at that cute baby penguin roll.
Adventure can be in your mind or in a book.
You can find them anywhere; would you care to take a look?

Darkness
by Grace Li

Through the fighting wars and the battlefield,
No trace of Peace alone.
Not once through the centuries did they yield.
Through the forests they have blown.
All loving signs perished from the wars.
Rage against the dying hope.
Every drop seeped through the cloth and out it poured
They fought through the prairies and through the Arctic slope.
The battles raged on and on,
The war destroyed everything in its path
A bloody red marks the rising dawn.
The villagers all the felt the war's wrath.
They hoped against hope that the war would stop.
The world's bond was falling apart!
The farmers were suffering, dying were the crops
Every soul striving; dying is one's heart.
The war ceased and halted,
But the darkness of the battles did not stop.

One Cartoony Night
by Theresa Perez

I remember that night, o so clear
When I first opened my eyes all I felt was fear!
Then I realized I was in Johnny Test
And well, then it all seemed like the best!
I hung out with Johnny and Dukey for a while
Then we ran from Susan and Mary's monsters for a mile
But then I realized I was at a row of cars
Then saw I'd run into Martin the Martian on Mars!
Me, Martin, and friends all partied together till we fell down
But I screamed as I kept on falling down, down, down
I fell down into snack time on Yoshi Island
But all the Yoshis, they still were smilin'
I loved to flutter-jump with them,
Soaring through the sky counting 8, 9, 10!
But then I fell from the sky with quite a start
And found myself in Mario Kart
The starting light counted down red, yellow, green, GO!
My car blasted away and I screamed WHOA!
I sped right through an unseen crack
Then I woke up as I hit the floor with a whack!

Basic Life
by Jaida Thompson

To put things simply, life isn't fair.
You are born, you grow, you work, you die.
Life can be filled with hardships
but you find joy in your work. And there is nothing
more satisfying than a job well done.

My Pet Parrot
by Sahana Darbhamulla

My pet parrot flies everywhere day and night
He has many colors that are very bright
He bites a number of times each day
That's the thing that I try to delay
His favorite place to rest is the stairs
If you manage to shoo him off he will be full of despair
He is very playful and loves to dance
It would be great to see him if you have a chance
He talks very loudly all the time
He is an intelligent parrot that is a wonderful mime
My parrot is an amazing friend
My parrot and I have a friendship that never ends

I Want Everything
by Anabeth Hylland

Ooooh I want everything the world has in its haands.
It would be great if I won one hundred graaand.
I want a puppy and a kitten,
one that will not steal my mitten
and I'm really hoping to succeed.
I want all the new top toys,
oh no, here come all the boys.
I better run so they won't steal my needs.
I mean, wouldn't it be cool if I read every single book.
It would be even better if I had my own Nook.
I want everything the world has in its haaaands.
It would be great if I won one hundred graaand.
I want all the gadgets and gizmos.
All the candy, all the clothes.
I want everything the world has in its hands.

Why ...
by Emily Olach

Earth ... why ... why are you round?
Earth ... why ... why do you spin?
Sun ... why ... why are you so hot?
Sun ... why ... why do you have rays?
Moon ... why ... why are you so bumpy?
Moon ... why ... why are you gray?
Why why why?

Sun
by Angelina VandenBosch

The sun is yellow
For the day
Now play, play, play
The sun is the most important!
It keeps you warm!
It keeps you healthy!
The sun keeps plants growing!
Helps the orbit circular!

When the Breeze Blows
by Mikayla Tegen

When the breeze blows, the leaves start to whirl and fly to the sky
And the branches sway from side to side
While the flowers move this way and that way
As if they were starting to dance and the bids were the singing choir
When the breeze start to blow, the clouds start to move
And change their shape from a circle to a giant clover in the sky
Then the breeze blows on every single butterfly
And makes them spread their wings wide so that I can see all the colors
And all the things that you can hear,
The trees moaning, groaning, and wailing,
As the dogs and wolves start to howl as it blows,
Sometimes it brings rain, which can make their noses wet
The wind can do and make so many things
Like stealing balloons or make ripples in the pond
The wind can take you farther than beyond in a hot air balloon
The wind does so many things for all sorts of animals
As it blows through my hair, I think of all this.

Dogs
by Samuel Manning

The dog was so cute
He was wearing Bogs too
He was so awesome

I'm Talking Earth!
by Autumn Graham

I'm talking Earth,
I'm talking people's land and water
I'm talking Earth,
I'm talking beach, sand, lakes
I'm talking Earth,
I'm talking road, cars, trucks
I'm talking Earth,
I'm talking school, teachers, kids
I'm talking Earth,
I'm talking big, green, blue,
I'm talking Earth,
I'm talking delicious food, horrible food, and in the middle food,
I may be talking all these things, but really I'm just talking plain, old Earth!

The One Man Band
by Elizabeth Ross

With the drum strapped on his back and bells on his fingertips
The One Man Band plays all of the instruments he equips
Wandering around the grimy dark streets
Humming and singing to the rhythm of the drum beats
A Horn on his shoe sounds whenever a step is taken
And the accordion he's holding also helps with the music making
People open up their windows to witness the act
Because the One Man Band is definitely back
They stare at the strange sight
But the band keeps pushing with all his might
Booms and honks are heard all over town
For everyone to hear this inspiring sound
He brought bright smiles to their faces and joyful thoughts to their head
For this music kept people's spirits alive, but it wasn't just what he said
The point was that the One Man Band was out there working so hard
To make people happy without asking for a credit card
He is certainly not the best of the best
But the passion he holds puts others to the test

Birde
by Randi Force

He flies in the sky,
the beautiful sky.
Oh, so high in the beautiful sky.
He seeks his love and fame,
looking for a wise and beautiful dame.
What is his name?
Birde, very wise I proclaim!

Spring
by Grace Hurst

Snow Melts
Geese Come Back
Animals Return
Rain Comes
Flowers Bloom
Trees Blossom
Grass Grows
Rivers Flow
The World
Wakes Up

Werewolves
by Serena Roth

Hungry for flesh
Grey, white, black, or brown
Razor sharp teeth
Huge sharp claws
Really hairy and soft
Mean and vicious
Long jaw
Huge long ears
Wolf like body
Wolf eyes
Colossal paws
Massive fluffy tail.
Strong and fearless.

My New Hair Bow
by Rachel Vander Meer

Mrs. Esman bought me
a pretty pink and white hair bow.
The ribbons twist like a pretzel.
The clasp grabs my hair and hangs on tight.
Yay! Thank you!
I said as she placed the beautiful bow in my hair.
I am smiling from ear to ear.

The Boy Who Loved Rainbows
by Jack Ambrogi

There was a boy who loved rainbows
To draw and to paint
So much you might just faint,
To collage
And to sketch.
He wouldn't play ball or play catch.
The boy who loved rainbows was
Always doing the same thing
Drawing rainbows,
What do you think!

Milo, My Cute Dog
by Ester Mills

Milo, my cute dog has floppy ears
and two big brown eyes.
His tiny wet nose sticks in my face
when I tie my shoelace.
He jumps up and down
when I come home from school,
But sometimes he's stubborn
like a little mule.
On one Friday evening
All dark and gray,
We found out that Milo
Had soon passed away.
Ever since that dreadful day
I never dared to love a dog
The same way.

Evil Teachers and DJs
by Harrison Deur

some teachers are mean
some teachers are nice
I suspect Mrs. Braymer is nice unless she's on her iPhone
let's go to the teachers lounge
there's a secret door behind the vending machine
and Mrs. Drake is the bubble queen when she won the DJ contest

Price Tag
by William Martino

There's a price tag
Hanging with a number
Sometimes high, sometimes low
You think "What else matters?"
But no, it's not about the machine
That prints all the green
It's about the people who spread red
Try that instead.
The healthiest, richest man on earth,
You may think he truly spent his lifetime well,
But the poorest, sickest man on earth may not
Have had the longest life or had everything
But if he had love,
Then he truly
Spent his life better.

My Teacher, My Hero
by Destinee Wonsey

Teacher says
Teacher knows
Teacher smiles
Teacher goes
You give your effort every single day
You might not have superpowers
But your care for the students is evident
Your lessons are effective
You're a role model for all
Teacher says
Teacher knows
Teacher smiles
Teacher goes

Indianapolis
by Aggie Koutz

Big towers
everywhere
traffic traffic traffic
hotels everywhere
people on the go
jobs jobs jobs
people are busy
but people
are still grateful
for what they
have

My African Praise Poem
by Ruby Giancaspro

Ruby
Behold a sun, a gem
Born in a foreign country
Chinese Zodiac, Spring Rolls, Grapes
Dancing, waiting to show the world
Friendly to the deer
Strong as the horse
An elegant swan leaping onstage
My rescuer, my companion, my dog
Dancer, athlete, lover, friend

Rainbow
by Kayla Vine

Red, orange, yellow green,
blue, and purple
it's a rainbow.
Wonderful colors in a rainbow
I love rainbows so much.
At the end of a rainbow is
a pot of gold.
Double rainbows
have double colors.
I love rainbows so much
rainbow, rainbow, rainbow
I love them.

Winter
by Selena Britton

My birthday is in winter
It's fun to play around
When we go outside it's stormy out
Until you hear a laughing sound
If you ever see a snowflake
You know it's winter time
Why don't you go sledding
And sing a little rhyme

A Grey Mouse
by Alec Snow

There once was a grey mouse
Whose only friend was a grey house
I know it sounds wrong
But he lives in Hong Kong
And he brought his beautiful spouse

Friendship
by Zohra Baig

Friendship is a drip of magic,
It isn't tragic,
It doesn't travel in a spaceship,
It travels in hardship,
Friendship is a drip of magic,
Which travels in a steamship,
If you speak bad language,
It will travel in an airship,
It will whip you with its grip
Friendship is a drip of magic,
It travels like a disease,
But a good disease,
Friendship's blip flies around the world
Bringing peace upon the world,
Friendship flips the people upside down,
A way to bring friendship upon the grounds.
Friendship is a drip of magic,
The most beautiful thing for friends.

The Car
by Tommy Yonan

I saw a car,
It went far.
It was red when I went to bed.
Now it's blue,
It just flew.
Whoa, it's green!
It is very mean.
I saw a car,
It went far.

America the Beautiful
by Alexia Love

America, America, as beautiful as it can be.
We have singing birds and lovely trees.
We have mountains, lakes, and valleys too.
If you only knew it was true, I would be willing to show you
Laughing and giggling, freedom and fun.
The sun shining in the light, before you know it will be night.
Twinkling stars dancing in the sky, they're like diamonds floating by.
America, America as beautiful as it can be.

My Dream
by Pranav Balasubramanian

A cardiologist is what I want to be.
My patients will be very happy to see me.
I think being a cardiologist will be exciting.
When I see the flowing blood it won't be frightening.
I know my parents will be proud of their son.
And talking with my patients will be lots of fun.
I am only a child, but I want to be well known.
Chicago, Ohio, Indiana– everywhere I will roam.
I will teach my patients how to take care of their hearts.
Their bodies will get a healthy new start.
I will be happy when I do a good job.
When I finish, around me I will see a big mob.
This is the dream that I want to come true.
If it does, I will never feel blue.

Bored
by Kaisee Jonio

I am so bored on a Saturday
All I want to do is go out and play
It's the middle of May
But yet it's been raining all day
I might as well just go and lay
Because I can not go out and play
on this Saturday!

The Plant
by Erica Bengel

Relaxing is how his days go.
Sitting by the window, waiting for a drink.
No one knows his feelings, no one knows his ways.
Like he is on vacation, all he does is stay.
Sitting by the window, just as he should be.
That is how he spends his days, happy as can be.

As the Lilac Blooms
by Brynn Sullivan

As the lilac blooms
and the mist on the sea
I'm all alone except the shadow
of me.
As the lilac blooms
and the tall mountains look
grand
In the middle of it all, I
stand.
As the lilac blooms
and the rain is soft and wet
"Is it just me ... alone?" I fret.
As the lilac blooms
and the forests grow
"It's not just me!" This
I know.
As the lilac blooms

Seasons
by Diya Dani

Summer, Spring, Winter and Fall,
they are the best of all.
In Summer in the sun,
we have lots of fun.
In Spring the flowers bloom,
and sun shines in the room.
In Fall the leaves fall from trees,
and honey is sucked from bees.
In Winter it's really cold,
so you better not be bold.
These are all my reasons.
Say hooray for seasons!

Teacherian
by Cara Stevens

This is a teacherian.
Teacherians live in a tough tunnel of terror in Tennessee.
Teacherians eat turtle teeth and tarantula turnovers.
Teacherians like teaching tiny children,
they also like talking to tarantulas.
Teacherians wear hideous tights with tacky turtlenecks and tiny socks.
One teacherian tickled me and touched my tiny tongue.

Smart
by Pierrah King

Smarter than Thomas Edison
who invented electricity so that people can have light and more
Smarter than a college professor
that has been there for so long that everybody knows him
Smarter than Malcolm X who memorized a whole dictionary
Smarter than a calculator
Smarter than a bird making a nest out of twigs for his home
Smarter than a parrot that talks and sings
Smarter than a computer that knows everything
Smarter than Alexander Graham Bell
who invented the telephone so everyone can talk to everyone
Smarter than a cell phone that calls people all over the world at any time
Smarter than a GPS that knows where every place is and knows how to get there
That's how smart I am!

Earth
by Madeline Hanchin

Everything as we know it
Air that we breathe
Rocky Mountains
The Oceans
Humpback whales

Grandma
by Mohammad Muntakim

Old, nice
Looking good.
Pretty as a rose,
Love her so much.
Far, Far away,
Like to see her,
Miss her too.
Happy love.
Happy memories.
She's my Grandma.

The Law
by Ofelia Yeghiyan

The law is so fragile
like a mirror,
or the water of the lake
which, with one touch, will easily break.
The mirror has a rim made out of solid gold,
and that is what the criminals are, so told.
The gold is so hard to break,
while so easy to make.
While the inside is made of light,
easily breakable glass,
A very large mass.
In night you can see it
shimmering in the moonlight.
Gentle as water.
A criminal breaks in
and shatters the mirror
into a million pieces.

Jesus Is Risen
by Noah Aleo

Joyful
Earthquake
Savior
Universe
Sinless

I am
Seven sacraments

Rabbi
Is always with us
Shepherd
Everlasting life
New life
 -Jesus saves

Rivers
by Rachelle Veal

Rivers are usually fast.
I love rivers.
Very long.
Endless flow.
Rivers are pretty.
Sometimes rocky.

Best Friends
by Aimee Daly

Be a good friend
Enjoy every moment
Say nice things
Trust them

Find nice times to remember
Run and play together
Imagine things
Every time counts
Not a minute strays
Depend on meeting new people
Stay friends forever

Moon
by Cameron Roloff

Moon is smaller than the sun
Only the Earth has life (not the moon)
On the moon, there is no air
No life is on the moon

Saturn
by Margaret Sheets

Soothing rings around me
As I rotate the sun I imagine it rotates me
The huge universe makes me a flea
U stare at me I stare at you
Really I'm not sure what I will be
Never more, never less, I'm Saturn and that's that

Alan
by Alan Cushing

Athletic in sports
Loveable all the time
Artistic with my grandfather
Nice a lot

Witty when I'm happy
Intense in football and soccer
Lover of my family
Laugher when told a joke
Interesting when I tell people new facts
Animal lover
Mathematical when problem solving

Cat lover
Unique person
Strong whenever I need to be
Happy when I'm with my family
Intelligent in school
Nauseous after spinning in circles
Giver at Christmas

Earth
by Reylin Sladics

Every waterfall flows beautifully
Atlantic ocean and many others are as blue as the sky
Rivers and streams make fantastic noises like music
The land is amazing in every way
Hot as the sun the beach is where you want to be

Hunter
by Johnathan Rascol

Hunter's tracking, found a buck! Now gun's cracking!
Under his arm, he carries a buck!
Now I help him clean the buck, yuck!
That hunter looks familiar to me
Even now he looks related to me
Right I was! That hunter is my dad!

Women Who Changed the World
by Tony Salamah

There were many women who changed how life goes
So we thank these women from our heads to our toes.
Rachel Carson stopped the spreading of DDT
And Curie won a Nobel Prize in chemistry.
Ella Fitzgerald was a music sensation,
And Harriet Tubman helped slaves across our nation.
Sally Ride orbited through heavenly spaces
And Sandra Day O'Connor handled big court cases.
There were many women who changed how life goes,
So we thank these women from our heads to our toes.
Amelia Earhart took a solo flight,
But Susan B. Anthony spoke on behalf of women's rights.
Rosa Parks fought about sitting in the front of the bus,
And with that she kept segregation from happening to us.
Valentina Tereshkova was the first women in space
And Maria Montessori let children work at their own pace.
There were many women who changed how life goes,
So we thank these women from our head to our toes.

3rd Place

Sanjana Mendon

Winter In My Country ...
by Sanjana Mendon

On a cold winter morning
I stared out my window
Rocky mountains were snuggled
With a white blanket of snow
Crystal snowflakes fell lightly
On my porch
The sun peaked timidly
Behind the puffy clouds
Slowly and slowly taking time
The sun came out
Melting the snow
Leaving puddles of icy water
Around the house
How beautiful it is
Living in my country

2nd Place

Daniel Penney

Sun Over War
by Daniel Penney

The sun sets over the fierce battle,
not paying mind to the praying of warriors
fallen below on the scorched soil,
which went from calm, sunny meadow
to fierce, bloody battle.
Unique, beautiful flowers
crunched to dust by retreating soldiers' boots,
and the never-ending hail fire of artillery
creating this wretched place.
The soldiers curse,
some pray,
some weep for longing of their loved ones.
But some are driven by fiery anger,
wishing not to mourn friends and family alike,
but to avenge them.
Both the mourners and avengers wish for this conflict to end,
as the sun watches over.

1st Place

Molly Schuh

The distinction of being this year's youngest winner,
and one of our most descriptive authors as well,
goes to Molly Schuh.
Molly writes to us from the third grade
and clearly shows a gift for creativity
that is nothing short of magical.
Well done, Molly!

The Magician
by Molly Schuh

His cape is the open galaxy
Free with stars for all to see
His wand is a lightning bolt
With booming thunder that never grows old
His black top hat is magical
Filled with comets that are wonderful
His playing cards are constellations
Seen flying through our observations
His juggling balls are the planets and on them you can see
Soaring above the Earth and clouds, flying, is me

Division II

Grades

6-7

It's Coming
by Makenzie Griffin

As the snow fell,
Down,
Down,
Down,
The bears fell asleep,
The deer ran as they leaped,
And the snow wrapped
around the valley,
Like a crown.
It's coming.
A blanket covered the shivering pines.
Cold,
Cold,
Cold.
The moon cast upon the snow,
It was an undisturbed show,
And the death-cold air froze
the lakes.
It's
Coming.

Morning To Night To Morning
by Jaclyn Swiderski

Single piece of grass, bent over,
One drop of dew, hanging on till fate evaporates it
West is still dark but east is lit by a golden sun
The birds are waking with the day; a gentle wind brings the afternoon
Strong river weakened by the newfound breeze
A cloud covers the yellow ball of light known as our sun
Rain is here and the sky dims
All is quiet till the graceful, agile deer comes to greet the dark
Wilderness and now stars are out,
Shining light onto the world like the beams of flashlights
And as we sleep a full moon rises then falls
And the sun arrives;
Now a single piece of grass, bent over …

Sports
by Jake Pappas

In the world there are all sorts
Like tennis, swimming, or basketball
You can play them all
They make you sweat
You can bet
They can keep your heart healthy
Or it can make you wealthy
I suggest sports to anyone
Trust me it is fun
You can play any day
Even if it is a rainy day
I play sports because there are all sorts

Resplendent Supernova
by Emilie Siclovan

Flares of light abound her body as grand stars burst in her eardrums,
Stardust coats her fingertips,
She is exceeding the state her soul was left in,
Time has incited her mind to finally travel forth,
She embraces the other side as the resplendent supernovas ignite her pathway,
She is dauntless as she journeys fleetingly through the aurora,
Slowly fading from the spotlight known as Earth's eyes,
Her body as loose as a feather;
She whispers her goodbyes to the pedestal she was once frozen upon,
She knows no restraints for she was once an anvil marooned skyward,
The Celestial Bodies so foreign to her wakeful eyes,
What is now her domicile was once an unexplored, virgin land
That had taunted her greatest fears,
She was lost, gone, frozen; a ghostly shell of the girl she once was,
All she encountered were the night skies teeming with thousands
Of twinkling stars, the yellow jewel of night
And the manner in which her loved ones sat
Beneath them as if she weren't even there,
She would scream out to them but they never heard
And the realization sent her into a spiraling tailspin,
She no longer could exist as they did,
Instead she would eye the night skies
As she clawed her way through the Milky Way,
She'd balance the equilibrium of Earth and Mars upon her shoulders:
Praying for normality,
Until the day she finally detected the voices crying out to her,
They had been crying out for so long

No Limit
by Caitlin MacVarish

Every once and a while you may doubt yourself and say
that you will never achieve your dreams
Failure is always on your mind, and your mental emotions are at the extremes,
Confidence is key; it will help you along the way
It may be hard at first but the benefits will always stay,
Don't be afraid, because you are limitless, and can soar across the sky
You need to spread your wings and learn how to fly,
Nothing is impossible, you have to believe you can, and try your best
Things will seem difficult, but it's just God's test,
The world will always go on, and there will always be a tomorrow
But you have to live everyday like your last,
so your life isn't filled with regret and sorrow
You are empowered with the will to succeed
To claim victory, you have to have positive emotions lead,
Know that taking risks is what life is all about
Believe in yourself and never doubt!

New Beginnings
by Ramya Chigurupati

The flowers are swaying lightly in the first breeze of spring.
They are slowly unfurling their petals, eager to join in the first dance of spring.
Carried along on a breeze is a story of faraway lands,
Of places where there is golden dust, and where there are snow-capped peaks
Also carried on that same breeze is a whirlwind,
A wind of fears, of disease, and of shattered dreams,
Fears striking the hearts of every being on Earth,
And because of this breeze, no one noticed the crackling golden glow,
Slowly creeping up farther and farther up the meadow,
The flowers didn't notice as they shriveled up and burned,
Losing their luminosity and color, as they became black
And all that was left was a charred field,
The rain came and washed away the ash, leaving the dirt fresh and moist
And there, something incredible happened,
A single bud, a vibrant green, popped out of the soil,
A promise of things better, of things bursting with life, and of hope,
Every day brings the promise of new life,
After all, do you stop believing in the sun at night?
There is always hope, no matter what happens.
And often times it is the only thing that you have left.

I Love My Mom
by Taaliyah Grayson

I love my mom, she really cares
I love my mom when she always shares
She sparkles and shines out the night
I love my mom when she turns on my sister's night light
I love my mom, she's really sweet
I love my mom when she dances to the beat
My mom's pretty, in and out
I love my mom, that's not a doubt
But the most thing I love about my mom
As you can see
That I love her and she loves me

Why Boat?
by Caroline Sisson

I am the ocean, free as can be,
But you are the one who disturbs me.
You boat!
Why do you hurt my waves?
Throwing things into them like they are graves?
Why boat?
Why do you pollute?
You even use my body to trash things like boots!
Who boat?
Who tells you to?
Hurt my body the way you do?
How boat?
How don't you know?
That I have feelings too, Though I just flow?
Where boat?
Where did this start?
Or am I just saying these words from my heart?
Stop boat.
Stop what you do.
For soon my body may not be blue.

That Is the Question
by Madisyn Danner

The children were running around
As the creaking silence of age echoed through the streets.
All the children who were running around have evacuated.
Or maybe they've just disappeared.
But why have they disappeared?
That is the question.
Why did they leave without a trace?
Why?
They used to tie ribbons in trees and swung from the branches.
There was nothing left, not even a single hair,
No footprints, no nothing.
Every second that ticks by, the children are screaming.
HELP!
Why do we hear their screams?
Did they really leave?
Or are they just hiding?
Maybe they're just playing a game and we're the seekers.
Maybe
Where have all the children gone?
But are they really gone though?
That is the question.
Nothing was left, no footprints, no blood, not even a hair.
Why can't we find them?
Maybe they'll never come back.
Or maybe they're just sleeping in rooms full of emptied shelves.
How were they emptied?
That is the question.
Maybe were sleeping and they're in the other room.
But why would we dream this?
Why would they leave?
That is the question.
Why did they leave without a trace?
Not even a hair was left.
How did they leave and why?
Why?
That is the question.
Where have all the children gone.

Will the Sun Ever Rise Again?
by Isabella Roselli

The sun sets into the darkness
before the day is done
The light fades over the horizon
like the last breath
The flowers droop and mourn their loss
and animals enter sulking,
waiting for predator to take them
in a dark depression
The moon is full and gives light
but it is not the same
it is trying,
unsuccessfully,
to cover the pain
The question rings in everyone's head,
"Will the sun ever rise again?"

To Be a Butterfly
by Phebe Gault

I sit and I think,
on a bright summer day,
the breeze whispers by,
I try not to blink,
as a butterfly lands on my finger.
Flutters oh so softly and sweet,
I don't dare to breathe,
so it won't fly away.
I'm so quiet I can hear my heartbeat,
the sunlight lands on my skin so warm,
I smile.
It turns and flaps its wings,
for I say goodbye,
I watch it, fly into the distance.
What would it be like to be a butterfly?
Flying to the sky to say hello to the sun,
as the clouds pass by.
I would feel free.
Just to be me.

The Man Really Liked His Pants
by Gracelyn Wilson

There once was a man from France.
He wore lots and lots of pants.
He got hit by a bus.
Then he made a big fuss.
That old man really liked his pants.

A Hobbit
by Isabel Holloway

A lazy hobbit in his hole
soon to have his story told.
When 13 dwarves and a wizard knock at his door,
the poor hobbit ends up leaving his hole.
With a ring from Gollum's cave,
and a troll's sword,
the dragon is defeated!
But only 10 dwarves,
a hobbit, and a wizard remain.
When the hobbit returns to his hole in the hill,
he finds an unpleasant surprise,
most of his items have been sold!
He was thought to be dead but here he is,
with his pride and story at his side.

Come With Me
by Madison Sewick

Come with me to the top of the world,
To the white snowy peaks,
Where you see the people gracefully sliding in steep u formation down the hill
And feel the chill of the brisk air against your raw skin,
Tasting the lingering burntness of hot cocoa,
You'll smell the smoke drifting from the chimney down the slope,
From the top of the slope you hear the gleeful screams of tricksters
soaring to the stars off the ramps just beyond the lift,
But only if you ...
Come with me to the top of the world, and escape reality
Come with me, and see Pure Michigan.

Down the Hall
by BryAnn Piot

Danger is my bully
She walks down the hall
Boys run when she does call
The blows she strikes me with, make me fall
I curl up in a ball
The pain never stops
Even as I walk home
I am alone
My limbs feel like stone
O I hope there aren't cracks in bone!
Why does no one hear?
Why does no one care?
I sigh
I let teardrops roll
They are a never ending river,
With a never ending flow.

Marauding Mane
by Grace Nolan

Lying on stones,
Protected by mother,
Depending on others,
A cub gains independence,
Being pushed out of home.
He grows and grows and grows.
Then one day,
He changes.
From cute
To strong.
From small
To a tremendous beast.
Marauding through grasses,
Pouncing atop victims,
Protecting his catch,
Living his lackadaisical days,
Bathing in sunshine,
Yawning,
Showing his sharp, white teeth,
Encircled by his ominous mane.

Operation
by Lucas Bell

They took me in
They strapped me down
They ran a bunch more tests
He showed much fright
We could see him shaking
We had him take a rest
I opened my eyes
I felt so good
The weight was off my chest

Lies
by Zachary Senko

One dark lonely day,
a sliver of sunlight appeared.
It washed the darkness away.
But there was still something that was still feared.
It slithers, it slips, it gets bigger and bigger,
'till it comes out you lips.
It then leaves.
But not for long,
for when it finds the keys,
it shatters silence like a gong.

Alex, Friend
by Caitlin Sivak

We loved each other
His long, white fur
Her gentle hands
We loved to sleep together
Invite each other to sit
In the cranberry sleeping bag
In her lap, warm and soft
Then,
Then,
The unfortunate sadness transpired
We had to part
Forever
Forever

The Myth of Old Times
by Alisha Saile

So maybe you've heard the myth of old times.
It's scary like witches but happy like fun times.
No one will get it and no one will change it,
It's crazy and wild because only horses can arrange it.
I never thought I'd see the day when someone cracked the spell
And the myth was no longer a myth, it was REAL!

Gone
by Brendan Osentoski

They used to be everywhere down there.
Now they are vanishing.
Like ghosts through a wall.
Demons, Attackers, Burners.
Chopping, hacking, burning.
Roars, caws, howls.
Locusts, Attackers, Burners.
Dark, desolate, empty.
Sooty black crisps.
No speck of green.
Demons, Attackers, Burners.

Fall / Autumn
by Jenna Lyman

Fall, or Autumn, whatever you call it.
Leaves changing, orange, red, and brown,
F
a
l
l
i
n
g
to the ground,
far, far, far,
on the dark green grass,
that smells so fresh,
and damp with dew.
The leaves get fragile and make trees bare,
as they fall far in the Autumn air,
leaving homes to say goodbye.

The Angels
by Mary DeVos

The Angels led you safely home to your resting place.
Home sweet home is where you'll go.
With all your love ones gathered 'round.
We wait to see you face to face.
No one can see your presence now.
but we still love you as the years go round.
No one should feel the pain you did,
that's why you went with Him to live.
We'll never forget you and all you did.
You always knew just what to do when patience was wearing thin.
This is why we miss you and everything you did.
In Jesus name Amen I say
with him you'll stay
until we meet again.

The King
by Muyang Wang

There was once a good, old King,
He would conquer a new land every spring.
One year he decided to take a big chance,
And try to conquer the powerful Nance.
He thought he would meet fierce opposition,
But that was only a superstition.
For once he crossed the sacred border,
The only problem was internal disorder.
He thought that this was all a joke,
The Nancians would retaliate if they were provoked.
So he waited until he saw many foes,
He thought, then I can deal a lethal blow.
Whenever he was ready to assemble his killers,
He always saw more Nancians banding together.
He knew he had a weapon that could demolish,
So he waited to do the most he could accomplish.
The King waited and waited for many years,
Until one day came his greatest fears.
The Nancians came with one attack;
The last thing the King heard was one big thwack.

The Beach
by Kayla Fitzpatrick

The beach is so nice
The waves are so beautiful
The sand is so nice
The sunset is so pretty
I can hear the kids playing
It is time to go

Another Day
by Jessie Greatorex

Drip, drip, drip
goes the rain
drizzling down my window
Another jaded day
Drop, drop, drop
There's no sign of sun in the sky
Only an army of gray clouds
Drip, drop, drip, drop
It is still raining
It seems as if all the drops are in a race
to get to the sleety, solid, slippery ground
Then I thought
I got an idea
I got on my rainboots
and grabbed my umbrella
Splish, splash, splosh
I ran outside and jumped in a puddle
Now I love it when it rains

Autumn
by Natasha Wilcox

I love to feel the autumn sunlight streaming down my face.
I love to feel the silky autumn roses in their vase.
I love to crunch the autumn leaves, for I love their reddish hue.
I love to gaze at autumn sky with shade of cobalt blue.
I love the straw-filled scarecrows grinning at the sand.
I wonder if they've noticed the crows perched on their hands.
I love the pumpkins, full and plump, they make good pumpkin pie.
I love to draw in autumn frost and watch the birds fly by.
I love autumn. I run and play. My breath puffs out in steam.
The only thing I do not like perhaps is Halloween.

Running
by Jack Laws

You may have fun.
You may be scared.
You may be going somewhere.
Are you being followed?
Are you following?
Are you looking?
Did you find something lost?
Are you going away from there?
Nobody knows but you.
But running cannot help those,
Those that have ran too much.
You cannot run from everything.

Seasons
by Preethi Kumaran

Seasons are different, and unique.
ach with different characteristics and different needs.
They are each beautiful and special in their own way.
The snow is melting, As the flowers are blooming,
Bringing happiness and joy with it.
Spring is a wonderful season, The flowers and colors being the reason.
The petals of the flowers are as smooth as velvet,
And as soft as the clouds in the sky.
The wind howls as if it was a lion roaring, Through the dark night sky.
As the summer begins, Starting off with a bright blue sky
The sun shines as bright as a light, While children laugh and play.
The long grass, Tickles your feet, As if it were little pines.
The beautiful leaves glows, Showing all their different colors,
Which brings delightful sight to our eyes.
The autumn leaves blow through the air like a dancer spinning.
The colorful leaves fall to the ground like feathers.
The wind blows, Sweeping the leaves like a broom sweeping dust.
The cold and chillness creeps behind your back like a snake stalking its prey.
Snowball fights and snowmen, Which brings the bliss to the children
The days are shorter, And the nights are longer.
Snow falls as light as a feather, Covering the ground like a thick white blanket.
Seasons are wonderful.
Seasons are great.
Seasons are one thing that likes to go their own way.

Snow
by Hannah Ulman

It goes on forever and ever,
It never stops,
It's been here forever,
When will it go away,
It's cold and wet,
I weep and weep
because it won't ever go away.

Sailing In the Sun
by Sophie Rogowyi

I watch the water glisten and gleam as I sail through the peaceful calm waters.
I lean over and feel tiny splashes of aqua blue water hit my face.
As I tighten up my main sheet I begin to heal the boat.
As I turn the tiller I quickly duck my head so the boom doesn't hit me.
I began to feel the wind whirling against the cheeks of my face.
I watch out for bigger boats as I gracefully glide at the water's edge.
I feel the thrill of excitement go through me as I sail my day away.
Dreaming of my next adventure, that awaits me the next day

A True Saint
by Ryan Lenaghan

Happy and bright
he never put us in a fright
he was like a ray of light
that never displayed his might.
My heart towered so high but then crashed to a low
O' how could such a man go?
So he departed for the gates of heaven
having a better life than someone 111
his cup was half full but never half empty
because he touched so many
Bill Fallon was an amazing person who should be in Bible verses.
Some days I ask God why, but he is so high
Silently listening in white clouds so glistening
While I mourn I feel no scorn
because I know Bill Martin Fallon is with God

Dinky Dapper Deer
by Joshua Brown

Dinky found a dapper deer in the delicious forest
He took it home and named it Dale.
But his dad did not want Dale.
So back to the delicious forest for Dale it was.

The Queen
by Mary Katherine Kozak

Once there was a queen,
Who was not very keen.
She was like a dancing fiend,
And liked to eat beans.
This might seem scary,
There was a fairy,
Whose name was Mary,
Who helped her with dramatic scenes.
Now you know about this strange queen,
And all the horrible things that I have seen.

Imagination
by Raul Dutta

Imagination
Like the mind's assertion
The spirit's stance
The dream's prance
One's creative resolution
Like a picture of the mind
That we so often blind
When we are young we paint on
When we are older the picture will be gone
Now the pictures have gone from us and we, from them are confined
Or did we leave them like a shepherd forgetting the sheep
The sheep will be gone when the shepherd is asleep
When we wake, is it too late?
We wonder if this is all part of fate
The answer is, it is never too late to leap
Leap into imagination
For, it is your own creation.

Summer
by Kimmy Moore

Summer is a hot season.
Summer is really wonderful weather.
Summer is when you eat a lot of ice cream because it cools you off.
Summer is when you can lay out to get a tan.
Summer is when school gets out.
Summer is the season for swimming.
Summer is the season for vacation trips.
Summer is when you have lemonade.
Summer is when you have parties and sleepovers.
Summer is when the pretty and wonderful flowers come out.
Summer is when you work out in the yard or outside.
Summer is a happy and fun season.
Summer is when you wear shorts and sleeveless tops.
Summer is when you wear sandals.
Summer is when you can relax.
Summer is when you hang out with your friends.

Journey
by Enrico Colón

The blissful scent is in the air,
A utopian universe; small as a hare,
I cannot cry,
I cannot sigh,
Oh what a happy place!
The odd stench of this dystopian place,
Beneath a united, peaceful race,
I cannot smile,
I cannot laugh,
Get me out of this place.
Like purgatory on the Earth,
I see no torture; yet no hearth,
No comfort here,
Albeit no pain,
It seems like no one belongs anywhere.
Although everyone has their faults,
We can't let this pull us apart,
We must defend,
We must protect,
Our dignity and respect.

Recital
by Chloe Brittain

Dress like ocean in the sun
Hair all perfect in a bun
Shoes that tap and then a slap
She shivers from fear and looks in the mirror
But she is ready; Fearless she says
Then the MC announces
The stage lights burn
And she shows what she has learned

Oh No!
by Maggie Paré

Oh no, I am in trouble now!
I woke up and guess what I found
My dog eating my homework
Oh no, my teacher is going to be mad when I tell her about this.
I don't know what to do, should I bring my dog to school or what?
All I know is to run before she calls me up to her desk!
So wish me luck
because I'm going to need it a lot!

Daughter To Mother
by Morgan Slater

Mother, please listen to me, while I tell you this:
Mother dearest, mother so sweet and so loved by me,
I can't imagine my life without you ...
When times are tough, you make it seem so easy.
In the midst of our unspoken love– trust ... honesty ...
We make great strides
You are the roses when they are red,
You are the color of my brown skin that– covers me,
You are my right and left hand,
You are everything about me.
You are my light when I am in the dark,
You are my fast when I am slow,
You are jazzy when I am classy,
We have so much in life to be thankful for
'Cause you are the best of times in the worst of times.
Mother dearest, mother so sweet and so loved by me.

Support
by William Thompson

some will support you.
most will ignore you.
and if you're my queen I will adore you
for all my life even through the strife,
forever and ever

Is
by Alyssa Richards

The silence seems to laugh in my face
A cold mirthless sound in this frigid tomb
The condensed drops of water hold my black and white memories
A past I cannot face and cannot forget
The chart hangs in my mind
A white bed of rock feels my back down for weaknesses
The place wants to break me
I cannot be broken
The only dent in a century I felt long ago
a break in my unbreakable armored soul
Tears cloud the drop that is that memory
If I could caress each loving cheek once more
My fingers and hands stay immobile in this cursed tomb

Why
by Angela Honeycutt

Why should we have to go through pain.
Why our life can't be the same.
Why we can't walk the streets at night.
Why we can't live right.
Why we have to lock your house down before we go to sleep at night.
Why can't a lot of children can't eat.
Why us blacks can't learn nothing or try to get an education.
Why us blacks can't work together as a nation.
Why, Why, Why. Why is the world like this.
Why does the world exist.
Why does the world got to be like this.
Why do we do this to each other.

Tornado
by Jordan Kurniawan

Dusk
I travel along, sucking up my food
I spin and spin, only to get dizzy
I suck up my dessert,
I leave destruction in my wake
But I am a gentle giant
Placing eggs gently on the ground
I grow sleepy with each passing minute
I fade into nothing when I am done

Spring
by Sierra Aguilar

The first sign of spring,
like someone at your doorbell,
DING!
The green isn't seen,
beautiful, silent, listening, and glistening.
Spring
A powerful beauty, not seen to the eye,
but like honesty, will never lie.

Eagle
by Sydney Weber

Flying, flying, flying free
up,up, up
above the great blue lake
soaring, gliding, flying,
resting in the treetops
the Mighty bird of prey
above the great blue lake
BANG!
plunging
down, down, down
into the icy depths
the mighty mountains looming above

Gummy Bears
by Tamiyah LaGrone

My brother loves gummy bears.
He even sticks them in his hair.
On his t-shirts and on the couch
He puts them all in a pouch.
But I prefer them in my mouth.

Winter Snow
by Dean Bellmore

Winter snow, so white, so bright, so soft
Oh how I love the color white
Plowing and snowmobiling
Making a snowman
Soon we go inside and have some cocoa
Watching the snow
Fall down like a mist of rain
Soon our tracks will
Fade away like
They were
Blown
Away

Gwen and Emily
by Mackenzie Baird

They are my friends oh so sweet
they laugh always on repeat,
If you wanna know
I love them so.
When you say goodbye
it's another puzzle piece you gotta find.
In the dark I knew they were there for me from the start.
When and where everywhere
I know they are there.
If you wanna know
I love them so,
It would be hard to let them go.
Gwen and Emily, you are sweet
I love the way you guys laugh on repeat.

The Dance
by Yu Yao Lovick

A flying leap creates the music
it drifts to space on air.
Eternal.
The wind flashes by like lightning in a storm.
The sky lights up the clouds of hope.
The stars dance.
The flowers sing.
Hands clapping,
wildfire through the crowd.
The whisper of a rippling leaf.
Silence.

Escape
by Josephine Henvey

Bookshelves, bookshelves, to the floor.
Bookshelves, bookshelves, to the door.
Bookshelves, bookshelves, here and there.
Bookshelves, bookshelves, everywhere!
They fill my home, they're filled with light.
They fill my heart, they fill my life.
My precious books, they make me gape.
My precious books are my escape.
Picture books, novels, chapter books and more!
My rooms are filled with books galore!
Tear stained pages, happy laughs.
The smell of dust on those pages will last.
Throughout the years! They smell so nice.
They get me through the days and nights.
The heroes and heroines, so brave and full of heart.
Literature is my favorite form of art.
So when I'm sad, or even bored.
I go to those book filled boards.
And escape to some far off land.
I'll always be fine, as long as there's a book in my hand.

Boom!
by Joshua Henderson

I feel dust and wind thrashing against my face.
My feet are hanging in the air.
I see lightning violently crash against the ground.
Buzz, boom, crash is all I hear.
I sense the shock of electricity chasing me.
I run for my life while the thunder thrashes.

It's Just You
by Meghan McKenzie

Love, something that you feel when loved back.
Life, it's just starting.
Courage, the thing that makes you, yourself.
All these things put together,
Makes a courageous, smart, person.
Nobody is too perfect, and nobody can be perfect.
Just being you is great.
Because it's just you.
Nobody can take it from you.

I Found You
by Jerrin Harvey

Somehow in this great big world
I found my way to you
My heart, my soul, that's who.
You make me smile.
You never fail to talk to me
Each and every day.
Whenever I have hurried home
With something, I must share,
I find it just so for comforting
That you are always there.
Encouragement you give me
And a friendship that is true.
I'm glad my soul while reaching out
Found someone like you.

What Friendship Means To Me
by Jade Brown

Friendship is a gain in life and I don't mean in pounds.
It's a warming in people that are all around.
Friendship is a special feeling that lies deep in our hearts
It's kind of like a play with all the leading parts.
Friendship is not something we should take for granted.
It's a feeling that lies deep within and often is enchanted.
Friendship means so much to me that nothing can compare.
To the wonderful smile it brings about that I really love to share.

Panic
by Islay Hepburn

A trickle of blood runs down my chin and onto my brand new white blouse
I panic, scary thoughts fill my mind
another drip,
d r i p
drop
d r i p
drop
I run into the empty bathroom
Three, two, one
I open my mouth, afraid of what I may see
as blood pours into the once cream colored sink.

Shall I Go
by Amelia Dogan

Who am I?
That is the question we all strive to answer,
The person walking,
Is that me?
Or am I just one of the seven billion people on the face of earth,
Am I at all important?
Should I believe that I am special?
My parents just suppress me,
It feels that my existence is just a problem,
I just want to leave,
Will I ever have a chance to break the bonds that hold me to this dreadful place?
I cry out to the desert.

Tornado
by Jack Anderson

The tornado,
rips through,
the defenseless countryside,
some things get picked up,
some things get thrown down,
some things just stand there silently and frown,
suddenly,
the clouds open,
light pours in,
and the tornado,
just can't sustain,
most is put back,
and people leave with pain,
the victims wait patiently,
only to be told,
that the light will grow old,
and the pain will return again,
bullying.

The Twin Towers Battle
by Maya Girschner

Did they know their fate
That soon they would fall,
collapse to the ground,
had no chance of surviving
They put up a good fight
There were two of them
They were twins ...
The battle begun
Two against one
It was obvious who was going to win
The last fist was thrown
They crumbled to the ground,
burst into pieces,
fought to get back up
But they stayed on the ground
It was two against one,
Not a fair fight
They tried with all their might
But today still
They haven't stood up

Floor
by Lillian Mitchell

The floor, no one cares
I'm always stepped on whether I'm cement, carpet, or wood.
No one loves me. I have no friends. I wish I had friends.
Would you be my friend?
Everyone throws trash at me, like I'm the trash can.
The floor, people please be more respectful to me
your friend, the floor.

I'm a Hockey Player
by Zachary Dotson

I'm a hockey player,
With ice in my veins and fire in my heart.
I think a jersey is high fashion,
Stanley is synonymous with sacred,
and icing isn't just for cupcakes.
My team is great
My team is strong
In net is a brick wall
The players are as weird as they get.
Go Night Hawks!

Football
by Jose Sanchez

I love football, it's my favorite,
some people may hate it.
My football number is number one,
being that number is lots of fun,
every time I play it makes me happy the rest of the day.
Football is a well known sport,
I play it with kids of every sort.
While playing football you can get hurt.
The reason I love football is the rumbling of the stands,
gets me fired up for game time.
When I put my helmet on it's game time.
When we walk on the field we are ready to win.
I get in my position and I am ready to play.
My love of the game is as much as my skill.

The Moon
by Austin Strong

It shimmers at night.
It's in outer space.
It's in the shape of a circle.
It's the moon.

The Soldier That Never Came Home
by Kendra Lang

You left me on that cold, December night,
when you went along to fight.
You had a stern look on your face,
Like you were going to race.
I wish you came back that night,
Or at least by the morning light.
I can't tell you how much I miss you
I hope you miss me too
I wonder if you'll ever come back
If not I'll have to pack.

My Girl
by Ah'maun Berry

Her beautiful brown hair, it's red at the tips,
Her beautiful eyes and silky smooth lips,
She melts me like butter on a hot summer day,
We'll always be together, that's what I say.
If I were a ghost, I'd be with her all day,
If she were a car, I'd drive her away.
Her beauty, it goes much deeper than an ocean,
She's my cupid, with the magic love potion.
Though I am young, I am capable of love,
She's an angel sent from Heaven, from Heaven up above.
I will take her to Paris, we will be in Rome all day,
When the vacation is over, I'll fly her away.
We'll fly to the Eiffel Tower, where I'll get on one knee,
I'll propose, and together we'll flee.
Till this day, we are still filled with glee,
Together we stay, my wife, and me.

Yellowstone
by RaeAnn Kievit

Spring in Yellowstone
Brings back many animals
Baby bison everywhere!

At the Pasture
by Cynthia Bauters

Going to get you, I call your name
You come galloping, thinking it's a game
You buck and buck, it's like you will never stop
And then suddenly when you do, I hear a very loud pop
A silver shoe comes flying through the air
I duck but it hits my derriere
I snatch you up and then the shoe
A bath is what you are due!

Winter Walk
by Maria Heeter

Wind brushes
glides through my hair
enveloping me
my chilled hands pull my hoodie
covering my mouth
in an attempt to stay warm.
Frozen, my legs blatantly struggle to push
through the icy gusts
that could blow a child
off their feet.
My nose lets out a column of frozen air
I sigh
reminiscing the freezing days
when my friends and I were dragons exhaling smoke
or breathing fire into each other's rosy faces.
Rotating my stiff arms
I walk up my front steps
awaiting hot chocolate and a fire
marking the end of my winter walk

Tick Tock Click Clock
by Ben Besteman

Time passes
As I lie in bed
A restless night
Twelve o'clock
The clock click clocks
Tick tocks
But I just lie there.
One o'clock
Still awake
I hear the mocking sounds of snoring
As I am awake
Tick tock click clock.
Six o'clock
My alarm goes off
Throughout the night
I couldn't even get a click of sleep.

Spring
by Olivia Hankey

The flowers are blooming everywhere,
For sure spring is here.
The snow is melting,
Putting an end to snowball pelting.
The days are getting longer,
As May comes our way.
With the cold days ending,
It's easier to go and play.
Every morning you will hear,
Birds singing newly born songs.
With no more icy roads,
There will be more toads.
With spring near,
I hope I see plenty of deer.
When I see the grown grass appear,
I know that it needs a good mow.
I can't believe spring is here,
It's my favorite time of the year.

The Boston Marathon
by Jett Ewing

April 15, 2013,
Why do people have to be so mean?
A Boston bombing has taken place,
And some people's limbs have been erased.
Some people had ran for a cause,
But the money is now for those who are wrapped up in gauze.
For the bombers that blew up the Earth,
I think you are scum and have no worth.
This travesty will never be ignored,
This killing is a story of pure horror.
The country is terrified, see what they've done,
A new era of mortal terror has begun.
Hearing the mourning of those who have lost,
And feeling the pain of the ultimate cost.
However, the worst sight of all,
Is watching the disaster of our country's great fall.

Spring
by Malina Gallmeyer

Spring, have you ever seen such a beautiful sight
Beautiful during morning or night
When the flowers say hey
And the kids want to play
Those are the best kind of days
When the clovers pop up
And the trees regain leaves
Where the sun isn't shy
And the snow says good-bye
When animals say hello
And snowmen say uh oh
Those are the best kind of days
The temperature is just right
And everyone is filled with delight
Where everything is okay
In the most brilliant of ways
When plants will thrive
And everything seems alive
Spring is what I want to see

Poetry
by Joseph Bicoll

It's all our teacher makes us do
It must be stuck in her head like a bottle of glue
It's so boring she must not like me
Man I hope she catches the flu

Weather Man
by Josh Ridder

If I could control the weather
I would buy a season pass to Bittersweet
And ski 'til I was a pro.
After that I might bright out the sun
And go fishing with my dad,
And for when I get thirsty,
I'll change it to the fall
And make some apple cider.
Of course I'll have to save some rays
For tanning in December!

Rota-Kiwan
by Tyler Kelly

I packed my bags, ready to go
Behind me, games and video
Ahead, five days of scouting fun
Camping, swimming, and summer sun
Day one, set up camp, what a mess
Ditched the 'rents, passed my swimming test
Fighting off bugs, mosquitos won
Collapsed in my bunk, end day one
Day two and three, merit badge spree
First aid, cooking, and archery
Camp songs, ghost stories have begun
Half the week is already done
Four and five were like lightning fast
Friendships and memories that last
Said my goodbyes, the week was fun
Now over, wish it just begun.

Head In the Bowl
by Mikayla Timlick

My head is stuck in a bowl.
I can't get it out.
I was scared they would cut
my head off
if I told my mom,
so I hid in my room.
Then she walked in and
I fell and it smashed!

Pencils
by Thomas Walker

Pencils are wood.
They don't have lead
But I think they should.
Pencils can write.
Pencils shouldn't bite.
Pencils can be long or short.
There are all different sorts.
Pencils can be purple or blue.
They can be sharp too.
Pencils last longer than a piece of wood in a fire.
But not as long as a shiny, new tire.

Chrysalis
by Lina Patel

On a quest for notes to sing my life's song
New growth and new hardship found every day
Help me find myself and where I belong
But where should I go and what should I say?
My views and my world– all of it's changed now
Watching my steps and trying not to fall
Want to find my place but I don't know how
Like a lost butterfly: lovely, yet small
I know the path, just need help getting there
Tunnels of mistakes and mountains of truth
I could myself– but the journey I'll share
Filling my role as independent youth
Yes, it's risky, I understand that well
But I'll be back soon with stories to tell

Chickadees
by Sydney O'Brien

Chick-a-dee-dee-dee
Chickadees are my favorite
Flying high and low

Sports
by Claire Alby

There are many different kinds of sports,
On the field or on the court.
We work as a team,
And that's every coach's dream.

The Farmers
by Lena Donajkowski

On a fall windy day,
The trees were swaying,
Side to side, left to right,
The kids were ready to play.
The farmers are harvesting hay,
While the farmers were harvesting hay,
There is still a bit of light,
The farmers were getting their pay!
The kids were playing in the hay,
The farmer was saying,
"It's getting late, good night!"
The horse whispers a neigh ...

Credo
by Alea Holloway

I believe in the bible, the things God says.
The gift of life is good.
The things we say, matter.
But I don't believe that life is easy.
I believe in cheaters never prosper.
I believe that truth comes to the light.
I believe in love at first sight.
I believe that love is a treasure,
That it brings joy, peace, and pleasure.

Ricky's Sticky Head
by Kristina Bellaire

There once was a young man named Ricky
His head was large, bald, and sticky
He got it stuck on a hat
Which was stuck to a cat
His days were just long and icky

My Family
by Kaitlyn Johnston

I have a family of four
One brother named Ricky
One mother named Elizabeth
One dad named Rick
and one dog named Zeus.
I have a big family
a family of five counting my dog.
I am happy to have all the members in this family
I have more in other families
on my mom's side
and my dad's side.

Golfing Is Fun
by David Weglowski

Golfing is a lot of fun
Hitting golf balls into the sun
Getting the golf ball onto the green
Is just simply keen
Golfing is not that easy
Your first time may make you queasy
But one thing I can't stand
Is getting the golf ball stuck in the sand
If you are an amateur like me, just start at the driving range
You really don't have anything to lose but some spare change
The one thing I think is frightening
Is golfing in a storm with a lot of lightning
Now if you get a hole in one
Now that is really fun
Then the people running the place will really cater
Because they will put your name in the newspaper

Race Car
by John Bullock

I'm a racer with a dream,
I wonder if I will make it in the big time
I hear my engine purr
I see my name in shining lights
I want to have it all
I'm a racer with a dream,
I pretend I am one in a million
I feel the rush of a million G's
I touch a dream
I worry if I will fail on national television
I cry when people are in pain
I'm a racer with a dream,
I understand I am great
I say, give me your best shot
I dream I win
I try my hardest
I hope, I believe I am right
I'm a racer with a dream.

My Kaleidoscope
by Alana Bonilla

Outside it bursts with color sensations,
It is as smooth as a sheet of silk,
It has designs that capture the mind's eye,
Inside beads clank and clatter,
While the different shapes share their unique qualities,
Patterns turn into ideas
If I sleep with my kaleidoscope under my pillow
I will dream the wonders of being a bead,
Spinning all around,
Feelings cluttered in this one contraption,
Light crawls through every crack and crevice,
My shape shines surely in one's eye
If I give my kaleidoscope to you,
You must care for it with all your warming heart,
You must realize all of its willing wonders
Without my kaleidoscope,
I will have a hole in my heart needing to be filled,
I will miss it with every last shard for my broken heart,
While it bursts with its color sensations

Haunted
by Matthew Wood

some say it's haunted
some say it's cursed
but the house at the marsh
is by far the worst

Love
by Sierra Warren

I wrote your name in the sky,
but the wind blew it away.
I wrote your name in the sand
but the waves washed it away.
I wrote your name in my heart,
and forever it will stay.

How Hot Is Popcorn?
by Alexis Wiskotoni

Popcorn, popcorn, how hot can it be?
I just found out 'cause it's popping on me!
Pop, pop, pop as it hits my skin,
Oh me, oh my, it feels like a pin,
That's why you never ask how hot popcorn can be!

I Tried
by Verith Long

I tried to catch a butterfly,
But I couldn't, why?
I tried to catch a star, but it was too far.
I tried to catch a rainbow,
And it was too bold.
I tried to catch a frog,
And it was on a log.
I tried to fly,
But fortunately I didn't die.
I tried, I tried.
I knew it took a lot of pride.
I tried ...

The Little, Big Lie
by Marshall Carlton

"Are we gonna go a bonfire?"
"But Dad, I'm tired."
But when the son went to bed,
That was the only thing in his head.
"DAD, YOU'RE A LIAR!"

Look There
by Konrad Lautenschlager

Look there,
Do you see it,
It croaks, jumps, and eats food,
If it could, it would escape here.
A frog.

Camping
by Jacob Marsh

Camping rocks,
Don't forget your socks.
You can catch a fish,
Or make a wish.
You can swim,
Also climb a limb.
You can ride a bike,
or catch a pike.

Imagination
by Peyton Miller

Imagine
Sirens ring with no noise
Tire skids with no marks
Fire as hot as the sun
Yet,
Could not burn
A man slipped, tripped, and fell with no cry
He sees his life flash by like lightning
The world feels sorrow as another life passes
But,
Tomorrow he will be back

The Perfect Game
by Ashley Pion

I throw 3 strikes in a row.
As I swing my arm as fast as a bow.
You might not believe what I have seen.
No ball was hit, especially past me.
I see the parents staring at me!
As the ball flings by like a little bee!
I get up on that mound feeling so proud.
While the other team doesn't even make a sound.
A girl's mom thinks her daughter is going to get a hit.
She couldn't have been more wrong as she missed by more than a bit.
This game was worth more than money for a chore.
No one could stop me now as I wanted more, more, more.
This girl got 2 strikes on me!
But then I hit a home run that went further than you could see!
We won by a lot to give them shame.
This couldn't have been more of the perfect game!

Gold and Silver
by David Elliott

You are gold.
I am silver.
You may be better.
But I am more common.
People get lucky when they find gold.
People are happy when they find me.
You are like a 1901 penny.
They barely find you.
Silver is like a one dollar bill.
I get used all the time.
People rarely find you.
When they do they get money.
People always find me.
Gold is like the sun.
Most of the time it is helpful.
Sometimes it is not.
I am always helpful.
They can use me for whatever they want.
Gold is like a president.
We rarely find a good one.
Silver is like a good person.
Which we find a lot of.

Cape Shore
by Fiona Houghtby

The waves break along the shore
And with them comes a gentle roar.
Seagulls fly above the burning sand
As the sun sets below the land.
The sailboats seem to drift away
As the night takes over day.
The grasses sway atop the dunes
And then appears the shining moon.
The seaweed floats without a care
As warm breezes blow through my hair.
While I sit in the cooling sand
Looking at shells in my hand.
Soon I hear the foghorn blow
And now I know that I must go.
So I walk back along the beach
Until my cottage I do reach.

The Magic of Nature
by Faith Carlson

It lies so true
In the yonderous pale blue
The clouds so puffy
And their puffs so fluffy
All of it has such a gentle breeze
Blowing through the tips of the trees
The trees are rustling
And the rivers bubbling
The water rushes
As it quickly gushes
The magic is more than that of a wand
As it rushes to the wide open pond
No grass is dry and weeping
The frogs there, all are leaping
The fish are all splashing
And quite so very dashing
The water begins glistening
Everybody is listening
It is quiet
Without a single riot

Florida
by Gabe Wiese

Here I am sitting in the sun
laying in a chair cooking like a bun;
Looking around people are being tanned
While I sit in a chair listening to a band;
We walk the beach all hot and warm
Nothing in sight not even a rainstorm;
The ocean was salty I didn't go in
Although I was hot I wanted to swim;
I head to the pool I need to cool down
I jumped in and swam all around;
We stayed till night and we played and we played
While the moon gave off a bluish shade;
We went to our room to go to sleep
Sooner or later I will be counting sheep;
I dose off in front of the moon
We have to leave tomorrow and that's the boom.

Reflections
by Angad Chugh

Time's flying, graduation is almost here,
It breaks my heart to say goodbye without shedding a tear.
The hectic, busy years went by awfully fast,
For me, school was a breeze, one happy, carefree blast.
My buddies and I studied, played and pulled pranks together,
I wish I could be attached to them forever, with a tether.
For my teacher and mentors, I will always have a special regard,
Their teachings and words in my mind, will never be marred.
I always wanted to be older and have more responsibility,
Now that I've grown, I wish time didn't go by with such agility.
Today, I look back at the years that have passed,
And reminisce the countless precious memories I have amassed.
I will treasure them and hold them close to my heart,
To lift my heavy spirits when I feel lonely and torn apart.
Tomorrow promises a bright new beginning, a new experience, a new face
Though, what I will lose today, time will never be able to replace.

A Coldhearted King
by Kelsie Kaufman

October is a cold-hearted king
with eyes of gold and red
He grips the earth
in his cold-hearted hand
and shakes it out of bed
He pushes you out the door
and surprises you with frost
He makes you gloomy and sad
happy to see you cross
He's mean and cruel
not kind at all determined
to keep his rule
But winter comes with white and peace
to take his throne away
Now we can rest in ease until
another day

Fly
by Nicole Byrd

To let go and fly
you have to be brave
like a tiger in the jungle
to let go and fly
you have to let go of the hand
that holds on to you
until you're ready to fly on your own
to fly,
fly,
fly
high up into the sky
to feel the breeze go through you
to let go and fly
just release your holding hand
you'll be okay
when you're ready, you've learned
what goes on in the world
so go ahead
let go when you're ready
I'll be here if you fall
let go
and fly.

Perfect World
by Katelyn Gerard

In a perfect world,
Kindness would surround us,
Judgement wouldn't exist,
Hatred would be dead,
Regrets wouldn't form a list.
In a perfect world,
Peace would be created,
Bullies wouldn't be mean,
Fights would become happiness,
Evil wouldn't be seen.
Our world isn't perfect,
But if it was, it could solve a lot of problems.
Wouldn't it be nice if
We lived in a
Perfect World.

Boom, Crash, Bang
by Jacob Brueck

I thought it would be easy
pedal, pedal, pedal
was all I could think
pedal, pedal, pedal
I thought it would be fun
Boom, Crash, Bang
I thought I knew how
wobble, wobble, wobble
the sign said stop,
stop, stop
I said go,
go, go
Boom, Crash, Bang
but now it hurt
pain, pain, pain
my dad said, "Get up", but I couldn't
man down
now one year
I'm back on my wheels
but faster and more courageous

Life
by Dominic Folsom

Ever think this amazing world is all a dream?
Ever think if the ground did not have grass?
Just look around you at this beautiful world.
But one day it shall all go black as you lay in a jar or maybe in a box.
You lay in that box never to awake.
You wake up one day not knowing of the other life you had.
Well, this is called "Life."

Roses
by Alana Stewart

Roses are red, violets are blue
I don't particularly like you
it's not that I hate you
but I'm not saying I love you
I just don't particularly like you
it's not your hair (like I care)
it's not your outfit (because I'm sure you will have a fit)
it's just I don't particularly like you
and when you think I do you say
we should marry particularly
and when you know I don't like you
you think I hate you and you cry
so, roses are red, violets are blue
I don't particularly like you

Cookies
by Caleigh Madej

Their savory smell fills me with joy,
chocolate chip cookies are fun to enjoy,
you could never make a cookie decoy.
Cookies are so yummy and sweet,
they could never be beat,
so chewy and chocolaty, I'm ready to eat.
I hear my mom pulling out the pans,
I wonder if she's going to bake a ham,
hopefully we don't have a cookie jam.
I heard the timer announcing the cookies are done,
they are so good, they are worth a ton,
the fun has finally begun.

Sunset
by Sarah VanDijk

Red and pink flowing
Deep darkness growing
The sun was sinking down
The gleaming ball of fire
Resting on the dark's wire
The sun was sinking down
Star's faces start to show
Shining as the white winter snow
The sun was sinking down
Day's last light
Soon to night
The sun was sinking down

Another Mary Had a Little Lamb
by Abigail Burnham

Mary had a little lamb,
Its fleece had many fleas to show
And everywhere that Mary went,
The fleas were sure to go
It followed her to school one day,
Which was against the rules
It made the children itch and scratch
To see the lamb at school.

Dreams
by Isabelle Thelen

DREAMS; no more than a thought at the back of your mind ...
... a DREAM, a DREAM
Where you are not who you SEEM to be
You are BETTER; You are MORE
Throw off humanity, like a chore
It is on DREAMS that we FLY!
Touching the birds and kissing the sky
On DREAMS do we SOAR!
In darkness and night
DREAMS break forth like hope and bring the LIGHT!!!
BANISH the DARKNESS bring forth the DAY!
Follow your DREAMS and find the WAY!!!

Candle In the Night
by Bailey Langbo

Candle in the window
Sitting on the sill.
Flame licking at the wick,
The only thing not still.
Orange core,
Outline of blue,
Yellow golden spike,
Blew out on cue.
So now it's dark,
No shine of the moon.
But the coming of dawn
Will come soon.
And there it is,
The light of day,
Appearing fast
And on its way.

Teachers
by Ryan LaFauci

Teachers are wonderful,
They make school worthwhile
Come in with their coffee and their apple
They always come in wearing a smile
Teachers are nice
They'll always be there for you
If you have to ask a question
Raising your hand will do
Teachers are supportive
They'll cheer you up when you're down
If you're sad about something, don't worry,
The teacher will always wipe your frown
Teachers get you ready
For what life brings your way
Teachers try to get you on track
And they get you ready for a future day
Teachers love teaching
They always have fun
They always welcome having a good time
As long as you have your work done.

Hercules
by Alyssa Madison

He's been around since I was tiny.
His coat black, brown, and shiny.
Always excited when I get home,
So we go outside and roam.
He loves to play, he loves to bark.
In my heart he left a mark.
His name makes him sound so big.
But he's just the size of a little twig.
As years pass,
We won't know how long he'll last
His hairs have grayed.
But in memory will never fade.
Some say he's just a pet,
He's in the family, you can bet.
He's just the same as you and I,
And I never want to say goodbye.

A Flower
by Alexander Kamal

The day a Tree first saw the Flower, beauty it held.
When he tried to talk, his words stumbled.
When he actually said something, he walked away, "Idiot," he mumbled.
The Flower was there everyday, making life better.
The Tree finally befriended the Flower, but he felt like, "This is a flower for me."
He vowed not to let this Flower float away, because they were meant to be.
The Tree, the Tree, that not many liked.
He thought that no one would ever care.
All the loneliness in that Tree, was almost too much to bare.
But when the Flower came along, he felt new again.
Like a new sapling, just planted in the ground of the Earth.
How the Tree feels now, is greater than his mother at the Tree's birth.
With the Tree and Flower together now, they are as happy as could be.
From the day they met, happy as they were, many doubted.
But from that day, a wonderful relationship had sprouted.
What a beautiful Lily the Flower is ...

Rainbow
by Kristin Maret

Red Orange Yellow
Green Blue Indigo Purple
In the pot of gold

Lost
by Mackenzie Bollman

Lost
Enter,
the maze,
I get lost
in the shelves.
I Wander
Until I find,
what, I am looking for.
What to pick,
I won't know,
until I've found it.

My Gift
by Skyler Leach

Christmas at Grandma's is really not normal!
In fact, it's crazy and loud, anything but formal.
Our family is really big, and still growing!
All the young kids excited, their toothless grins showing.
Opening shiny presents and lots of toys,
The little girls are excited, and so are the boys.
There is lots of squealing and giggles,
The children are dancing to "The Wiggles."
I'm thinking, in the middle of all this mess,
"Is there anything for me?" I confess.
My childish excitement is loading,
Like a Fourth of July firework exploding!
Finally, I look over and spy,
A beautifully wrapped box that says "Skye."
Can it be? I think so!
This gift is mine, I know!

Basket
by Darren McCaffrey

Basket
Soft, hard
Weaving
Makes a happy hat
Basket

Hole In One
by Brett Boyd

Swinging many clubs
I once got a perfect hole
Ready to get another

Untitled
by Alex Bellmore

Snow melts, gravel dries
Rain pours heavily from sky
Gravel wet again

Softball
by Corinne Cogdell

Softballs, softballs everywhere
Softballs, softballs in my hair
Everywhere in my hair
I think I just saw a bear over there
I'm at the plate, ready to swing
But then I heard a phone ring
I'm about to swing my bat
But then I saw a rat
There it was, the rat
At my bat
I said, "Shoo," but it said "Boo."
Then I heard a cow moo
But that's not it, I swung the bat
With the rat
And I hit the ball
To the wall

Pepto-Bismol
by Jake McNeal IV

Pinky
Winky
Bottled by
the double
Helping
stomachs
in trouble

Beef Jerky
by Jonah Sibley

I got some beef jerky
But it was quite quirky
Now I want some more
But I can't go to the store
Now I want some turkey

Christmas Love
by Ethan VanEnkevort

Silver bells are ringing,
My nerves are just a tingling.
Presents under the tree,
And all of them are just for me.
Christmas carols sang all around,
Everybody does a dance in town.
Making gingerbread men is fun,
Too bad we can't make a ton.
Every house strung with lights,
They are all such beautiful sights.
Winter clothes keep you warm,
To weather any winter storm.
When you come in from the snow,
You probably want a cup of Joe.
Snowflakes fall all around,
They violently hit the ground.
Now it is time to call it a day,
But tomorrow we will play.
There will be presents under the tree,
We will have to wait and see.

Cat
by Sarah Schutz

The cat, the cat put on a hat
and sat to rest on a mat.
The cat, the cat ate too much
so now the cat is fat.

Fall
by Rachel Ohrt

The high grass blowing hard
Leaves falling down from the trees
So beautiful, leaves

Raindrop
by Paige Rachel

Just from one little
Rain Drop
Everything was
Gone
From one raindrop to a
Storm
Flooding the World
No umbrella to protect me
Rain
    Still
        Falling
Lightning Crackling
Rain
    Still
        Falling
Until the last raindrop falls
And the world is still

Divorce
by Emily Walton

Devastating
Inconsolable
Very sad
Over thinking
Rethink about it
Calling names
Everyone lost

Everything About Mario
by Brandon Vu

"Mamma mia"
A hero of many
Ready for adventure
In the ride of his life.
On a quest to save someone special.

Grasping Dreams
by Allison Stein

I would get to the point
Where I would be grasping at my dream
Holding it in the palm of my hand
But then, well, things would change
The wind would shift directions
I would be morphed into someone else
I would lose my desire, my hope
I would lose my dream
But I never lost my dream forever
It kept coming back to haunt me
Begging to be dreamt one more time
To be imagined, to be envisioned
To be considered impossible
Something only inspiration could conquer
Someday, I would catch my dream
And I wouldn't let go

Change Will Come
by Erick Herrera

Don't ever give up
Because things will change
You have to be tough
Throughout the whole game
This may seem strange
But whatever is happening
Just smile throughout the whole range
And not care what anybody says
You might think you're different
But you're perfect
It's not you it's them
They should all get their eyes checked
And realize the beauty in you
They're the flu
Trying to make you feel bad
You're something that they wish they had
You might hear some whispers here and there
But take a deep breath
And just don't care
Because I swear that you're rare.

Furry Bunnies
by Priya Paray

Furry Bunnies in a house
Not much smaller than a mouse
Furry Bunnies sniff my hand
While I laid the fresh new sand
Furry Bunnies eating food
While changing from a grumpy mood
Furry Bunnies hopping up and down
While I listen to the soft sweet sound
Furry Bunnies, Furry Bunnies, Furry, Furry, Furry Bunnies
Furry Bunnies eating carrots
Never talking like a parrot
Furry Bunnies so cute so small
On their hind feet they are so tall
Furry Bunnies are super smart
And make a really cute, lovely sweetheart
Furry Bunnies not much to see
Luckily I have them all for me!

Friendship
by Jaylee Reynolds

Friends are someone you hold on to,
not to let go of
Friends will be there for you
whenever you need them,
Whenever you need them
they will be there.

A Door and a Key
by Alyssa Martinez

All you need is a door and a key
to open a new world for you to see
Life is good, life is great,
Live in your dreams, find your fate
Life is short, make it long
Let's all try to get along
Make sure to laugh, have some fun
Always know what you have won
And always know with all your heart
you have more time, this is only the start.

Best Friends
by Toni Iovine

A best friend is someone to laugh with
You can tell all your secrets to them
Best friends are the ones you talk to 24/7
Having a best friend is a gift only certain people get
And I am one of those people
They are the ones that are always there for you
And help you get through hard times
Best friends cheer you up when you're sad
They're always on your side
Best friends are forever
And should always be treasured
They are special to you
And have a big place in your heart
They love you and you love them too

3rd Place

Raelyn Whitney

Autumn Mirage
by Raelyn Whitney

Countless beads of amber
shot through with brazen gold
pinned to broad stalks of bronze
'til set free by the cold.
'neath the orange canopy
but o'er earth and stone
a dusky pool fills the grove
with a forest of its own.
It seems to be in summer
but darker, deeper hues
like a sliver of another world
a mirror we see through.
Its trunks are dark, and almost black
its leaves, a midnight green
but as I watch, the image fades
again an autumn screen.

2nd Place

Ekemini Nkanta

Freedom Flag
by Ekemini Nkanta

A colored canvas
speckled with stars
lined with the colors of freedom,
waving in a silent sense of justice.
Even as the towers tumble
and the bombs explode,
it continues to stand
eternally free.
We confess in a pledge
of never-wavering allegiance,
and with hands over our hearts
we remember what it represents
and the liberty it promises.
Maybe,
in a more peaceful world,
we can fly among its stars
and sail across its stripes.

Hallet Thalheimer

From the sixth grade
comes the creative work of Hallet Thalheimer.
With an obvious flare for expression,
Hallet's poem, "The Gardener,"
seems to blossom before our eyes
into a thing of beauty.
Congratulations, Hallet on an excellent poem!

The Gardener
by Hallet Thalheimer

He sits on a stone, the gardener
Hands ungloved, feeling airy loam beneath his fingers
Shaping it into something
Diverse. Effervescent. Exotic
He takes dirt, transforms it into aloes, cedars
Tall and imposing, menacing yet beautiful
Strong
From tidy rows spring lettuce, kale, Swiss chard
From a wild scattering, dandelions and apples
From the young girl, sunflowers vibrant and upturned
From the elderly, cabbage and peas
The sailor tends to his Brussels and beans, The aeronaut, his date-palms.
The widow, thyme, oregano, a sprig of rosemary
Just one minute acorn forms an oak. Just one trivial cone grows a pine
A gardener must linger, be persistent. Tend to his plot
Must water. Must aspire. Must trust
I am a gardener

Division III

Grades 8-9

The Life of Me
by Marquis Lewis

Life is a compass
Bright and full of light
Life is a change in your emotions
When the string is off, I turn back into a normal person
My life is like an empty soul, metal with thread
Life is a square, inside you feel lonely and down, only accompanied by four walls
Life is great, the string enhances motivation
Life is full of disappointments and dangers, the sadness surprises me
Life is the spirit of nature, it's cool and windy
Life is full of creatures marking all the time I've got.

Maybe
by Amiah Burner

I seem like an upbeat person. Most people don't like me for it.
After my father's unexpected death, I shut down, not talking, sleeping or eating.
That month I spent my nights getting high and my days barely sober.
Just to keep the pain away even if it's just for a little while.
I went to doctors and therapy and it helped.
I knew school would start soon, so I'd have to talk sooner or later.
Or I'd be more of an outcast than I already was.
The happier I seem, the harder it is for me not to cry
You have taunted me, even though I was nice to you.
You knew what happened and you continued to break me,
All because you don't like me.
I'm sorry you don't like me, because I do too much.
I'm sorry you don't accept me, but it's okay.
Because ... news flash!
I don't like you either, but honestly you made my life easier,
One less person to care about.
If I had a choice I wouldn't talk or even be here for that matter.
I'd be in a safe house ...
Driven to get better, but I'm better.
Because I'm here!
Don't feel sorry for me or pity me
The choices I made have made me stronger.
I've faced my demons and I accept them.
And maybe you
One day ... maybe

Sun
by Morgan Lecato

The sun shining bright.
Children playing in the grass.
Hot, warm summer day.

Sea Breeze
by Claudia Marques

The sun bears down on my sweaty face
But how I love to be by that sea place
The tall grass skims my hands,
And then I begin to feel a slight breeze.
I close my eyes and my mouth forms a smile
For this breeze is the sea breeze.
This breeze leaves tiny chills
All over my body and leaves me filled.
The sea breeze blows and blows and blows
As fast as it comes, it goes
For the sea breeze smells
Completely different from any other breeze.
And that is exactly why
I love the wonderful sea breeze.

Chair
by Nailah Mays

I am tired of being sat on.
A little worn out from all the big thumps.
Abused. Hurt.
"I need a better place to live!"
My owner has no manners,
the children jump on me.
I am soft like a baby's blanket.
You rock, rock all day long.
"Can I get a break?"
Even the wind bullies me.
Always pushing me around!
When is my big break?
Will I ever get a chance to just relax?
Too bad you're always doing it!
No fair, I think. Not cool. What about what I want?

What You Mean To Me
by Kylie Fritz

Your SMILE is like the ocean currents,
it pulls me in deeper and deeper until I am swept away in it ...
Your HEART is like the Sun,
it touches and warms me, unlike any other force on Earth ...
Your PERSONALITY is like the inside of a colorful forest,
there have been so many beautiful discovers within it ...
Your COURAGE is like strong boulders,
it has been tested by the strong winds of time ...
yet it does not wither ... it does not falter ...
My LOVE for you is like the universe, it is vast and never ends ...
YOU are like the air we breath ... special ... unique ... irreplaceable.

The Old Bridge
by Abigail Eberstein

About a mile from my house
Is a place that I feel at home
I've been going there for as long as I can remember
I'd go for long walks with my dad and dog
I couldn't wait to get there to play in the water with my dog
Now my dog is gone and I have grown so I walk alone to the place I still call home
The walk doesn't seem so long now and I don't play in the water
It's now a place I go to think to clear my mind
But even now from time to time
I stop to think about the good old times we used to have my dog and I
A place that I call home, a place just a mile down the road

Thunderstorm
by Shannon Lin

When will this be over?
The zigzagged flash of yellow:
glimmering, glowing, illuminating the Earth for only a split second.
The rain: howling, hollering, and hailing, it won't seem to stop.
Like a corpulent giant stomping through the streets,
the clapping thunder shakes the room, startling me every time.
I toss and turn and yearn for the peaceful nature.
Thunder roars and another one echoes,
like two people arguing over a dilemma that we never be resolved.
The rambunctious crying of the sky is still going strong.
Throughout the murky, gloomy night, I lay restless, eyelids wide open.

Please Stop Competing With Me
by Michelle Dorshimer

I promise you've already won
This is no longer fun
I beg just leave me be
Please stop competing with me
I weigh 40 pounds more than you
What ever you want you do
You're as beautiful as the shining sea
Please stop competing with me
You're supposed to be my best friend
I promise you set all the school trends
You make me want to move to another country
Please stop competing with me
I know you're insecure
But now it must end
You have to gain some confidence
Till then we are no longer friends

The Way Life Is ...
by Milan Minner

Life is great
Life is a clock
It's just a matter of time
Inside you feel
lonely and down
you get lost in the wind
Life is full of disappointments and dangers
Life is a change in your emotions
locked in mental rehabilitation
my life is like an empty soul
This string is from a happy place
If the string could talk it would say
tie me tighter
When the string is off
the only sound is the ticking clock
marking all the time I've got
stuck in the lonely state of mind
That's Bright and full of light

Untitled
by Keith Palombo

The cool wind blowing through my hair
The fans are screaming everywhere
There is a breeze on this cool spring day
I step into the batters box and the world around me seems to go gray
I glance at the pitcher as he stares at me
the base runners take their lead
The pitch is thrown, this is it
I swing the bat, it's a hit

I Will Never
by Taylor Guthridge

I will never trust the same fool again
that I called myself having a relationship.
I will not!
I will not ever put my emotion or time
into some young "punk" or "thug" that comes my way.
I will not ever in my life again put my confidence
and the way I feel about myself into no ones hand.
I will not make it
his job to make me feel beautiful or pretty.
And I will not, never ever, trust that same dog again
because he will never be worth my time.

The Lonely Chair
by Ava Boyd

Looking at the back of a chair, hoping for an idea to rise,
I see Sellin written in silver sharpie, even though I'm in Chase's classroom despise.
The chair has a hole, just perfect for my feet,
It's plastic and blue, it's really not that neat.
It's next to the window, where the fresh air seeps in.
With no one here to sit, the chair, lonely, just sits there.
It's quite sad. Thinking the chair is alone,
Made to hold someone, but has no one to hold.
Abandoned and old it sits ... alone.
Waiting for someone to claim it. When sat in, it squeaks and moans.
In a different world, new people come and go.
Thinking, "No one will claim me, and my good side will never show."

Justin Bieber
by Autumn Whetstone

I shine bright like a diamond.
Then I show up to the scene with my roof gone.
I am hot like a hot volcano.
I am famous like MJ.
All the girls run to me like it's raining money in one spot.
I am the most viewed person on Youtube
Get at me boy!

MLK
by Montel Anderson

Stepped to the mic,
Let your voice be heard,
You're like the king of the jungle,
They're all here for you,
Your voice, their ear, a sound wave connection,
You had a dream, we all do,
You can't see me, but I can see you.

Tragically Unfelt
by Kayla Sheehan

Tragically Unfelt
My soul is a black entity.
All I feel are my clammy cheeks,
tarnished from the abyss in place of my heart.
Broken from the man who selfishly abandoned me.
I am a million pounds.
Heavy from the scent of pine that chases me,
Whenever I close my eyes.
Heavy from hidden glares that trace me,
as I sit alone every Sunday morning.
And heavy from blood curdling tastes,
that eat away at my tongue.
I'm an unsolved puzzle missing one piece.
My heart tattered from the man that passed,
Whose laugh still lingers like a long lasting level of love.
Love; the butterflies I encountered when he kissed my nose,
And the warmth I felt when he handed me that blush tinted rose.
My skin aches for his silky warm caress,
That from now until forever will be left;
Tragically Unfelt.

I Love You
by Brandy DeLeeuw

Everyone is here.
Did you know that?
You can't go, you can't leave us.
The house is still,
and yet buzzing with fear.
I hear your rasping breathing.
Time has come to a halt and I know.
The room breaks down,
everyone collapses from grief.
We sing. "You are my sunshine"
What will happen without our sunshine?
You're gone, never returning.
I miss you already
I love you.

The Candy Shop
by Andrew Li

The smell inside allured my senses
But the choice has always denied my arrival
Change in my pocket rattled with ambiance as
My longing for something sweet was left unsolved
It was not the regret in my thoughts that deterred
Whether I could pick the right choice
But it was ending I wanted to become
To become the better end
The first candy I tried, gave me delectable taste
But it left me with bitterness in my mouth
Quickly reaching for another handful, the owner slapped my hand
Leaving a foul roll on my tongue
The second was disappointing compared to the first
Giving a faint, fruity taste that you had to focus on to enjoy
But it went on for a prolonged period of time for it to wither out
Like a fire smoldering in the wind
A warm tingle was left in my body
Followed by an energetic shiver
The door chimed as I made my choice
My choice of a better end

Rain Violet
by Miriam Ross

April's newest bloom
Born in a tender rainfall
Violet behind green

Deceive Me Not
by Juanita Townsend

Was it you or me?
To do me this bad, did I ever hurt you or deceive you?
Or was it me that stabbed myself in the back?
Love me or leave me but never let me go!
You see this smile on my face?
Have you felt the hurt in my spirit?
You see my face tells lies,
The look on my face will never tell what I've been through.
Not even how far I've came.
But sadly you judge me!
Why be so bitter? So cold?
I'm sorry! - I'm sorry for the mistakes I've made
I'm sorry for the times I almost didn't make it out of my struggle.
As often as I try to please you I fail.
What, when, how do I make you happy?
Yeah there were times I should've listened
But the devil defies me of the truth
I'm stuck and not easily found.
My life is like a carousel, it goes 'round, 'round, and up and down.
Did you know about the night I cried myself to sleep?
Hoping and praying to God I didn't wake to see the morning sun.
Or the times I looked in the mirror and saw nothing but disgrace.
The countless times I thought I had someone
To trust and they turned out to be my enemy.
Have you ever been so fed up but caught yourself in the midst
Because you knew there was greater!
Steadily all I do is press! Telling myself I will not fall!
Now when I look up I feel a shaking
I feel something moving in the spirit.
It's delivering me and preparing me for greater
As tears flow down my face, my body starts to tremble at will
I see a light, my break through, my redeemer
I see ... Love!

Love ...
by Kourtney Glaser

Love is said to be like a fairytale.
Makes you believe it's to last forever.
But does a fairytale ever have Non-Happy endings?
I believe not; Love on the other hand does
With Fairytales you always know the ending
With Love you never know how it is going to end
Fairytales were made to end happily ...
Love ...
Does anyone actually know how Love is supposed to end ...
Who really knows, because Love will either leave you happy;
Or on the other hand, leave you torn to pieces.
That's the difference between love and fairytales.

The Battle Brings the End
by Chantell Burrell

It's a nice day out but the air is so thick with tension you could cut it with a knife,
our enemies shooting pellets as blazing as the sun directly at us
aiming to pierce our skin with every shot.
PING! There goes one bullet popping off my helmet.
As I fight off one of the enemies, I look to the right ...
all I hear is BANG BANG BANG ! Down goes 10 year old James.
There it goes again BANG BANG BANG, louder than cannons.
Right there in front of me, my bunk mate drops down to the dark brown mud
with cherry red blood gushing from his chest.
The smell of his blood, piercing my nose as I sprint past his now lifeless body.
I turn around and I see the eyes of the devil himself.
In less than one minute I am not the one laying
helpless, defenseless, and lifeless on the ground.
Flashbacks of waking up early in the morning with my brother,
eating breakfast that my mother had prepared before going to school
come to mind.
My wife I am going to miss most of all.
Her hair, as brown as the mud I am now covered in.
Her eyes, bluer than the Atlantic ocean.
Her favorite yellow dress she loves so much.
Seeing her and my family are the things I will miss.
Soon I close my eyes and dive head first into an endless sleep.

Emotionless
by Elizabeth Crossley

Life is emotionless, so why try to deny.
People lie and say they love, hate, and feel remorse,
but the truth is we're all emotionless. But we try to hide
so stop hiding let your lack of emotion show & be yourself
& not someone else

Memories
by Alex Lopez

My friend's dad passed away today,
I don't know what to say.
He will have to live day-to-day,
Knowing his father has gone away.
At the funeral his father lay,
And I can only say
That he is in a better place,
As I look at the mother with tears on her face.
My friend asked why his father,
he could not take it any farther.
He began to spiral downhill,
There was now a hole unfilled.
I said everything happens for a reason,
And we do not know the season.
He was not listening,
School he began missing,
He was drifting from life,
He no longer could fight.
The next night,
He sat at where his father lay,
There he would stay,
For about a day.
Around him gathered a crowd,
The people mumbled aloud.
Then he began to say,
"There is no longer a reason for me to stay."
Then he walked away never to return to that place,
For he would remember his Dad with happy memories and grace.

Bittersweet Memories
by Raven Strefling

A heart is a heart,
Most people take them for granted,
Cut them, shoot them, gut them, whatever you please,
Mine has been through the ringer.
Has your heart been cut or shot?
Let me help,
I'm used to fixing them,
Worried about the marks? Don't worry,
Mine's identical.
A girl I liked deeply, put a knife in mine,
Then,
A back stabbing friend pulled it out the other side,
I stitch that wound,
Using these words as a guide for my needle,
I hope I don't make it worse,
In and out this needle goes,
Fixing it, for what I hope, is the last.

A Place Unknown
by Alexis Dietz

Past the pond and the old willow tree,
Down the path and across the creek,
Here lies a place, a place unseen.
Through the brawny trees the light will show,
Here the plants and animals are free to grow,
For this is a place, a place unknown.
Here in this place there isn't a sound,
Except for the birds when they sing out loud,
As they build their nest on this familiar ground.
This is a place where the animals roam,
This is a place they call their own,
For this is a place, a place unknown.
When people see this place they leave it be,
Because many may look but few will see,
This place's wonder, awe, and true beauty.
Maybe one day this place will not grow,
Maybe one day this place will be shown,
But for right now, it's a place, a place unknown.

Challenge
by Maitland Bowen

When faced with the oppression of the day
The iron fist, threat'ning infinite dark,
Cry out! Hold your head high among the fray
Raise your torch, raise your hand, sing with the lark
When fieriest souls meet most outraged minds
When the shining light refuses to die
The people join together, smash their binds
Challenge those that thieve from you your rights! Defy
The sly censor, suppressing the masses
Though you may tire, weary from exertion
Worn from fighting their many trespasses
Don't feel defeated by their coercion
The war against oppression is not done
With resolved will and strength, it can be won.

I Am From Cold Winter Nights
by Mikhayla Mowen

I am from "Hold on tight"
From my head and body getting cold
I'm from face full of snow
From fogged up goggles
From loud engines vrooming
I'm from hot chocolate before bed
From heating up in the garage
I'm from face full of mud from the ditch
From "Don't go too fast"
From getting run over by a sled
I'm from the quad's exhaust to bright lights in my face
From fuzzy socks to a wet hat
From freezing feet to bright red cheeks
From "We lost some people behind"
I'm from snow in my boots to
Bumpy rides from passing over the driveway to go around again to
"Lean to the right now lean to the left"
I am from cold winter nights

A Turtle
by Joseph Dessert

Turtle,
O, cool turtle
with your crusty green shell,
can go in the water and land
as well.

My Butterfly
by Erica Voorde

My safe haven is a place I have never been,
Just a fantasy, and now I wonder when.
It's really just a hopeless dream,
One that makes you want to scream.
Over the mountains and trees and lakes,
Now I realize what's at stake.
there's no one there but my Butterfly,
She glides on my shoulder when I cry.
She is my forever friend,
And forever has no end.
Gracious, beautiful, inside and out,
Friendship's what it's all about.
I cringe when she is not near me,
Forget the person I want to be.
She is my flightless Butterfly,
Friends forever– until we die.

The Cat
by Dominic Repucci

Sedentary on the chair, unobserved
The animal that we recognize as a cat lies dormant without a sound
Little do we know the capabilities of that particular feline.
The fluffy hair is as soft as a fresh washed sheet
Almost doubling the small tabby in size
Slow sleeping breaths move the dormant ball up and down like a crashing wave.
When the cat awakes, a new boldness becomes present
The cat pursues food, attacking and confronting everything in its path
Finally it catches its prey, and like a dinosaur it devours its prize.
The mouser begins a new search for a ray of sun
Like it's on a great expedition the cat ventures
When the objective is reached, it's time for hibernation, yet again.

Dragons
by Thomas Carr

Dragons are cool
I swim with them in deep pools
I can't help my obsession
It's just the brain compression
Please don't be so aggressive
Dragons have always been persuasive
They cannot be invasive
There is no competition
Just waiting for completion
Can't have just any reason
To have a dragon for the season
You got to have a dragon to love
To get a dragon first get have a dove
Don't live in an apartment
Dragons can't survive in small compartments
I got a dragon he is very caring
There is no way of sharing
Now to leave you
Dragons are like birds they travel in flocks
Now take a trip to the docks

A Wet Sky
by Rebecca Hoffmann

Are the tears you hold back, distantly connected to the ocean?
If you let out a small sigh, to let one raindrop fall, would it taste
like soaked, saltwater sand?
If I brushed away the slick tracks
that trace your cheekbones,
would a tide pool collect upon my fingertips?
If I looked closely, could I see the ripples and waves of the ocean in the rings
of your pupils?
Or hear the soft sigh of water rushing
up the coastline?
You are the sea, my love,
and I, simply an admirer,
who sits on your rocky walls to wait
for your cool fingers to glide over
my skin.
I wait for
the day when your waves reach me.

Butterfly
by Monica Davis

Delicately floating
Landing on a leaf
Moving to a flower
For long I will not stay
Bright blue wings
Flapping gently
Fluttering away
Before you can catch me
Flying to a new place
To land once again

Take the Plunge
by Sara Grubba

Dive into a book
If it's good, you won't want to come out
The story comes alive
The movie starts in your head
You start to know the characters more than your best friend
The plot gets intense
You can't stop reading until it's over
Then your life is too

The Sun
by Dustin Paad

The sun is beautiful with vivid color
With love and joy, with share of others
The sun is awake for the beginning of the day
But falls asleep the rest of the way
The sun is like a king watching over the Earth
And the creatures to whom the Earth gave birth
The sun is cool, like you and me
The sun also has emotions, like happy
During the summer, the sun is hot
Leaving some of us with freckled spots
With love and friendship on this day
The sun shines and lights the way
While we lay in our beds at night
We know the sun will always be there
With the moon and the stars as our light.

Backyard Friends
by Autumn Gratti

They come at sunset,
For their evening meal.
They come for their corn,
Before the birds can steal.
As I look into the distance,
I see a Mother and her babies,
They are so charming.
I walk out on my porch,
And I try my best not to be alarming.
Soon they will leave,
And go back into the woods,
But as they leave, I am certain,
I will see them tomorrow,
When I pull aside my curtain.

Love and Roses
by Alexis Wade

What is the symbol,
of love all around?
The most beautiful flower,
the rose is the crown.
Not a tulip,
nor daisy.
For the rose is the best.
Love is so beautiful,
you'll see while it lasts.
Roses are gorgeous,
yes that is true.
But there is another reason,
that I must tell you.
Roses have thorns,
something most flowers do not.
With love comes pain,
and with roses come thorns.
But it's worth it,
oh so worth it in the end.
When you find love, you'll understand my friend.

Free Candy
by Cassie Fitzgerald

when going to a party
be prepared for a piñata
because when it bursts
kids yell "yada! yada! yada!"
when you run around all dressed up
go door to door
like "was s'up!"
give me that candy, more, more, more
you have to say please
don't need no store

Darkness
by Joshua Gibbs

What darkness is it that teachers speak of?
Is it from down below or from above?
Was it hate or was it God's Divine Love?
You have more than one chance
But when you see the light of God you get a glance
And when you seek and you find you must advance
The Holy Bible is the key
To open eyes and let you see
The bright light of eternity

Early Spring
by Abigail Miedema

The world is weeping,
She is softening to your touch
up to the surface, her fingers push
Reaching, searching for the sun
To warm her frozen skin with life
She cries out
For something to cover
Her brown, dirty, empty side
Blanket of snow, return!
Or a new, softer quilt of green instead?
Why this turmoil?
Oh gust, blow in the spring
The world awaits

His Love
by Grace Gauthier

He looks over at me
His smile so bright, so full of compassion
If only he knew
He talks to me,
His words so sweet, so full of kindness
If only he knew
He holds my hand
His hands so big, so full of warmth
If only he knew
He kisses me
His lips so soft, so full of love
If only he knew, if only he knew
He gave me hope
He pushed me through it
He kept me alive

Lost Soul
by Robyn Caron

The pieces are broken all over the floor.
There is nothing left for me to fight for.
I am empty, empty inside.
My soul has left my body.
Abandoned.
No emotions left in me.
Stripped of oxygen, no longer able to breathe.
The beat of a heart, is silenced.
What am I now, besides emptiness
beneath my skin, inside my bones,
my fingertips have turned to stone.
A useless bundle of the old me,
being carried off, and buried.
I see it all, but I can't do a thing,
since I am just a soul with angry eyes.
They say it was suicide,
but that's not the truth.
Liar. Liar.
They should know
I was murdered by you.

Maybe
by Jessica Johnson

I stared blankly out the window,
And watched the rain fall from the seemingly sad sky,
Drop by drop,
My mind began to wonder,
Maybe life is really all that simple,
But we as humans insist on making it difficult.
Maybe love is really what's needed,
To make your whole world go round.
Maybe all you really need to do,
Is smile to be truly happy.
I search through the archives of my thoughts,
Wondering if I, myself have an answer.
I then close my eyes and smile softly.
Maybe this journey in life,
Is to find the answers to the most sought after questions.

Ten Little Kittens
by Tim Farrar

Ten little kittens playing ball,
One was taken by a bird, then there was nine.
Nine little kittens playing around the house,
One was taken to the vet, then there was eight.
Eight little kittens playing with yarn,
One got tangled, then there was seven.
Seven little kittens playing with signs,
One got smashed, then there was six.
Six little kittens playing tag,
One was it, then there was five.
Five little kittens playing Hide and Seek,
One got lost, then there was four.
Four little kittens playing with glue sticks,
One got stuck, then there was three.
Three little kittens playing with knives,
One got cut, then there was two.
Two little kittens playing with books,
One got a paper cut, then there was one.
One little kitten playing, then it was taken home,
Then there was none.

Sports
by Eddie Davidson

Football
Painful, fun
Tackling, running, throwing
Field, paint, yards, score
Catching, sliding, diving
Bruised, broken
Sports
Agonizing, mean
Moving, falling, bleeding
Points, weight, pin, pulling
Bruised, matched
Wrestling

Me
by Olivia Bertrand

Olivia
Artistic, responsible, devoted, considerate.
Sister of Heidi.
Lover of Bones (her cat), music, volleyball.
Who feels blissful, unrivaled, tuckered out.
Who fears heights, clowns, spiders.
Who gives smiles, advice, laughter.
Who would like to see Georgia, Florida, California.
Resident of Michigan.
Bertrand

The Pain Inside
by Kaitlin Fitzgerald

Tears run down my face, a mask covers the pain
Inside me from showing to the outside world.
No one understands my pain, no one cares about me.
I'm alone.
Isolated from everyone around me.
The pain never stops, still caged up inside me.
It never truly goes away, always a mark left behind.
Scarred for life.
Isolated from everyone around me, always a mark left behind.
Scarred for life.
Caged up inside me.
A pain that no one sees, always there with me.

Cold Stone
by Marlon Moore

At night there was a light brown stone sitting on the cold wet ground.
The raindrops pounded the hard stone like gun bullets.
The wind and air froze the cold stone.
Oh poor stone are you cold?
Do you need sand to cover you? Are you being stepped on?
The poor little light brown stone is being carried to the beach for sand cover.
And the stone is covered.

Fade To Gray
by Michael Harlan

Time runs its marathon,
Ending year after year,
Turning mountains to beaches,
Lakes to tiny ponds.
Changing us, and making us,
and growing us, and more.
So as the clock runs your final lap,
And familiar fades to gray.
Will you beg for one more hour?
Would you even want to stay?

The Past
by Emily Hiner

Love lasted little
Never a day,
Now I wish
It wasn't that way.
Deep in the bottle
I stayed my whole life,
Nothing occurred
But my knife
Blisters and bruises
Covered my scars,
Painting my body
Life a full out war
I took a deep breath
For it was my last,
Today is the day
I'll dwell on my past.

Laura E. Morris
by Alle Leffingwell

Laura
Generous, comical, artistic, deafening
Granddaughter of Laura
Lover of pals, pens, paper
Who feels fatigue, ill, unplanned
Who needs pain reliever, doodling, edibles
Who fears mice, grating, skin cells
Who gives support, giggles, attitude
Who would like to see Las Vegas, Marilyn Monroe, Jamaica
Resident of K-town
Morris

Cops, Crops and Mortar Pops
by Anthony Torres

Old McBrian wanted potatoes, Mary sent the crop,
but when the King sent calling, he sent the chop.
In the trenches Winston fought, him and Lee together thought,
how nice it'd be to get away, until the mortars blew him away.
There was a street punk named Mack, who was pulled over by the cops,
he talked some smack and got a whack, and now he lies under the rocks.
This little light of mine was a gift unto me
I'm going to let it shine you safely on your way.
10,000 days and the lights almost out.

Everyone's the Same
by Amanda Schlosser

People "hate" life
I can never be happy, no one really cares
But I still survive
People look but not see, at the mask I put on
I try to talk, but I am accused
Look very close, everyone's the same.
People "love" life
Pretending to be happy, everyone seems to care
But I never tell
I thrive in the eyes of people, but sink in my mind
I talk all the time, but loathe every word
Look very close, everyone's the same.

Summer
by Rudibeth Martinez

Summer breeze is in the air
Blankets of flowers all around
School is out, everyone shouts
Swimsuits and sunglasses?
We are off to the beach.
Blazing sun, it's just a ton.
Ice cream and smoothies with your friends
As you swim and relax with a magazine on your side,
Reading the new summer trend.
Fireworks and parties
With a nice smell of cookouts and BBQs
A breeze picks up, a red leaf lands on your plate.
Summer is always over, I just want to start all over.
Which in New Hampshire, it hasn't even started ...
Yet.

Your Secret
by Mikaylah Horn

Shut your mouth.
Hold it in.
Try to thicken.
Your so thin skin.
Take a breath.
Count to ten.
Don't let them know
You're hurt again.
If you're broken inside,
Keep it there.
Do you actually think
Anyone would care?
Stupid girl,
Don't say a word.
People may listen,
But you won't be heard.
Brush yourself off,
Put your make up on.
Don't tell anyone
Tomorrow you plan to be gone.

To Spend the Day
by Emily Simonis

Swirled hues against a pale sky,
Slight breeze through the trees,
As if you can fly.
Sweet melodies in the air,
Fluttering through the boughs,
Whistling as if not a care.
Rustling between the blades of green,
Creatures waken to the day,
Forever are they keen.
Breathe in the sweet scent,
As closed eyes see,
That's a day well spent.
Why not call your friends,
Laugh in merriment,
Friendship does not end.
Never a better way,
Peace all around
To spend the day.

Dreams
by Maple Xu

There are two types of dreams.
One is only achievable with a team:
You and that dream
Guided by that futuristic light beam.
Only when you believe,
Will you achieve.
The other dream occurs when you sleep,
Especially when that sleep is deep.
This type of dream is useless,
So think about it less.
The other dream, the first one,
Will get you your home run.
It will reward you.
It will reward you until you say, "Woohoo!"
So try, try, and try again,
Until you achieve that dream, like all wise men.
And that's when you know,
Your life was worth it, and you yourself will grow.

Just a Crush
by Matthew Barclay

Though I know she'll never feel the same
I bare no ill will against her
It's just a crush right?
I crave her voice and would like to speak to her
But I can rarely muster the courage to say more than "hi"
Whenever I'm near her, it is as though my body spontaneously combusting
So I've learned to take comfort in just observing her radiant beauty from afar
Like a silent guardian, forever watching
I'm constantly debating with myself
Should I attempt to approach her?
Should I try to initiate a conversation with her?
I always win ...
Forever longing for her warm embrace, to bask in her essence
Every time I see her it's like seeing her for the first time
Never a word but she leaves me flustered with emotions
It's just a crush ...

Beauty and the Beast
by Danielle Durst

Once there was a boy,
His eyes glowed like yellow gems,
He sometimes howled at the moon,
Refused to eat with forks and spoons,
He was different and alone,
And sometimes, after he had changed back on a cold night,
He could look up at the sky and call out to God, "Why?"
Once there was a girl,
Her eyes were as red as blood,
Her pale skin glowed against the brown mud,
That she threw her victim's bodies in when she was done.
Sometimes as the blood of her latest victim ran down her face,
She would drop to her knees,
Next to the freshly killed body,
Cry softly and look up at the sky and call out to God, "Why?"
Once there was a boy and a girl,
They were as different as different can be,
They looked at each other and fell in love
But because society had cast them away, they stayed silent
And were sad and alone for the rest of their days

Self
by Mackenzie Luck

Alison
Kind, Honest, Appreciative, and Hilarious
Sister of Mackenzie
Lover of Dance, Pageants, and Sparkles
Who feels Energized, Excited, and Happy
Who needs Family, Friends, and Dance
Who gives Knowledge, Encouragement, and Love
Who fears Spiders, Snakes, and Bees
Who would like to see Justin Bieber, Taylor Swift, and Bella Thorne
Resident of Michigan
Luck

Moving On
by Ashley West

Take a look around, seeing all the different faces.
Pale, dull, lifeless. They have not moved from their resting grounds
in such a while. We went to pay our respects, not to mourn.
There was already time for that. We move on in life, not by far.
It takes us some time, and some place where we can feel home again.
The dull faces tend to disappear, and the light faces show.
Enjoying life comes easier, and everyone seems happier.
Nobody is sad, everyone is enjoying the time.
Time is endless, and so are the ones you have shared it with.

These Dreams
by Melyssa Donovan

Red roses,
The sound of bagpipes,
Will haunt me always.
No one knows how I feel,
Not many people ever will.
The nightmares come continuously,
Whether I'm sleeping or awake.
I think of those brave people,
Who risk their lives to save others.
Rushing into burning buildings,
Never knowing if they will come back out.
That's what my daddy does.
For I am a firefighter's daughter,
And those terrible dreams will stay with me forever.

It's All In the Past
by Josie Marvin

Another day goes by,
Faces bring you to mind.
My heart is aching.
I try ... but the memories fade.
I stare at the old photos,
And tears start streaming.
So now I have realized
You were all I need.
Oh, how I miss you.
But you have died,
It's all gone.
I wish to see you,
Just one more time.
But then again,
I can't go back.
It's all in the past.

Sitting Here
by Elizabeth Kelly

Sitting here I saw many things,
But none stronger than those that sing.
Why do we sing even when we're sad?
What's the point when we're this mad?
Sitting here I had time to ask,
But who can I ask when we all wear a mask?
Time shows no sympathy for my condition,
It's on its own special mission.
Sitting here I was so confused,
But why should I be when I'm only used.
God has a plan for us all,
We don't know it though 'till we get the call.
Sitting here I took no blame,
But still God's not ashamed.
Everyone left me here alone,
Now my God has shown.
Sitting here I wanted to know,
But He only answered by telling me, "Go."
So I asked God for one more day and he gave me seven.
Then I asked for a home, he gave me heaven.

Changing Seasons
by Timothy Halloran

I sit and stay still
Only home the flower bed
Never will I leave
Roses in garden
Red, pink, white as well thorny
That's why I wear gloves
Green pointy soft grass
Grow tall and goes brown then dies
For the snow falls now
White sparkly flakes falls
Men made from the flakes that fell
I wonder why now
The sun comes again
Melt away all my fun snow
Still I love it all

Failure
by Margarita Lechuga

Sometimes you don't even try
Then you feel like a complete failure.
You try to impress the wrong people
When you should be performing for yourself.
You bring yourself down when people could care less.
You take stuff people say to heart and their words always scroll in your brain.
People think you're strong when you're really the weak link.
People think you will become nothing in life, because they think you're worthless,
and less than them.
People think you will always be there to listen to their harsh words,
or to be their second choice.
People think they know what is best for you
when they don't even have the slightest clue.
You try to fake a smile, and if people could only look past your eyes
they would know how you really feel.
So from now on it's a new beginning,
and let the tears you have shed wash away your past.
If you care about what people say and what they think about you,
you will never move onto greatness.
So when failure crosses your path,
you pick yourself up and fix those flaws to do better the next time,
but remember to do it for yourself and no one else.

Advice
by Alexandria Cutean

Don't start the virus
Bullying damages self esteem
Nobody likes a bully
Bullying is a contagious disease
People are hurt physically and verbally
Put a stop to the virus
Be the voice
Stand up for the victim
STOP! the bullying

Death of a Child
by Robert Blaisdell

Death of a child,
Whose mother was wild
With him in the car,
Pretty close to the bar.
A man in a truck,
Who was way too drunk
Hands slipped on the wheel,
Steel crunching steel
Crashed into a tire,
His foot twisted like a wire.
The mother turned her head,
And her child was dead.

The Forgotten One
by Emily Hubble

Can you find me?
You see I am not here, yet I am all the same
I'm the wind and the air
I am lost, that is true, but only to you
You look but don't see, like a blind man, could it be
Though if it's all the same to you, I'll wait until you do
I'll wait, watch, and hear, unnoticed, but not forgotten
I have but one request to make before I disappear for good
That every now and then, you'll look for me in my favorite tree
That you will stay and talk with me
At least until the count of three.

Leaving Him Behind
by Phil Engel

Her hazel eyes and coffee hair
Her unique and quirky sense of humor
Only make it harder as she pulls me into a hug
Her slightly greener hazel eyes and caramel hair
Her fandoms and impossible imagination
Will be something hard to find in any other
Her sapphire eyes and golden hair
Her small voice and cute, yet slightly dark personality
Add to the laundry list of reasons why I don't want to leave
But even after all that,
I think if I were to have one reason not to go,
It would be
His chocolate eyes and curly raven hair
His gentleness and tentativeness in contrast to his physique
His quick jokes and easy smiles
Him.

The Holocaust
by Isabel Tobin

The bullets shrieked through the air
The Jews screamed and fled
They ran for their lives, but the killing spread
They rushed through the streets that were covered with the dead
They were soon rounded up
The tears began to flow
The Jews were the friends, the Nazis the foes
Soon the friends were pushed forward they were forced to go
They were shoved into trains
They were tired, sick, hot, and had no food
They sat for days in their own stench and waste, it was very crude
Their situation was vile, and they were in a hopeless mood
They were pulled out of those trains
Pushed into the camps where most of them died
They were all important, the Nazis had lied
I wish they were saved but nobody tried

Seasons
by Lexi Wheeler

Summer is the time
For vacations, for tans
For chilling at the beach
For time with family
Fall is the time
For school, for soccer
For catching up with friends
For dancing leaves
Winter is the time
For skiing, for snowball fights
For the Holidays
For fires in the fireplace
Spring is the time
For flowers, for softball
For lightning storms
For gardening

Telling Me
by Kalimah Muhammad

I'm number one in my heart, I was here from the start.
People telling me to let it go! But my answer is always no.
I turn around to the world, and I ask in the mirror, who is this girl?
My head is spinning around. While my life is going down.
All the pain that I feel, is because of people not being real.
I see their lies in their face. I see them out of place.
I don't need them to tell me what to do, 'cause I don't want to be you.
Trying to be the best I can be. I don't need no one telling me!
She left me for you, because you do things she tells you to do.
I cry out loud for you to come in the light. But to you my future it not bright.
People telling me to be like you. But I can be great too!
They say, stand up and be right. But some tell me to just fight.
What should I believe? Who is being true? Because there is no more me and you.
There is no one by my side. Just the truth passing by.
Who can come in your place? Because there are lies in my face.
How can I be the best I can be? Who can tell me?

Lost
by Darby Stipe

Lost in the ocean,
Lost at sea,
Lost where no one can ever find me.
The biting wind blows,
The white waves crash,
The sky ignites with a sudden flash.
Too far from shore,
To ever be seen,
The ship is veiled with an icy sheen.
A torrent of rain,
Deafening thunder,
Nothing, it seems will ease it's hunger.
Lost without light,
The storm still reigns,
A flicker of hope is all that remains.

Our Dream
by Katera Fox

Good-night my angel, good-night my love.
Until tomorrow when we wake from the coo of a dove.
Tonight, I dream about you and me,
Sitting under our maple tree.
Enjoying our time together,
Before we have to leave forever.
You kiss my check, whispering
"I love you,"
I look at you and ask, "Is that true?'
"I will love you until the last star dies in the sky,
For our love will forever fly."
You say smiling, and slide your arm around my hips
Your kiss resting on my lips.
You hold me tighter,
As we watch the morning sun grow brighter.

Rain
by Dana Hiltunen

Dripping slightly, birds go hide
I see it coming, I run inside.
Raining harder, coming down
It seeps into the soggy ground.
Pouring now from the sky
I can't go play, I start to cry.
The rain eases up and so do my tears
Then it stops altogether, I burst out in cheers!
I put on my raincoat, my boots and my sweater
Then went tromping out into the weather
I stomp and I splash, I have lots of fun
I can't believe that the rain is done!
Then it went dark, I started to grown
In about thirty seconds I was soaked to the bone.

The Year of 3012
by Chittesh Thavamani

Global warming has taken over,
Temperatures shooting through the roof,
Ozone levels down the drain,
Those scientists of the past have been such goofs.
Animals dying here and there,
Extinction happening as quick as a wink,
Dead bodies of animals lying about,
The extinction of dogs is right on the brink.
There is no more color but that of the sands,
All of the green has turned into brown,
Sandstorms and Dust Devils wreak havoc throughout,
They engulf you with dust and leave you to drown.
This is the world at the rate we're going,
Mother Nature will die like a rat in a hole,
You have a choice and a role to play,
Prevent this from happening and make it your goal.

Hidden
by Hannah Powless

I think mean things inside my head
Terrible things never to be said
They stay inside for my mouth never opens
To leave sad feelings and all hearts broken
No, these feelings are tucked inside
Undisturbed and safe to hide
Hurting people is not the way
So hidden these feelings are going to stay
In a corner out of sight
Camouflaged to do what's right

Why
by Isaiah Welch

Why am I the one being beaten time after time
While you're not embarrassed but you're safe and sound.
Why am I the one being pushed and tugged even though it shall break my bones.
Why am I the one coming with a shallow insides.
Why am I the one being that has a broken heart that repeats itself
Every breath and move I make it will bring me more trouble
And I earn more pain.
When the shadow looks down upon me it looks in a stubborn way.
Now I have these chains around my ankles, you will whip me repeatedly
Saying bow down before me. I will still carry the marks of a wounded solider
Acting being integrated behind enemy lines.
Why am I the one acting like it hurts constantly bring cruel dark shallow pain.
After a while you what seems to be a tear dropping down my face
It hits the ground like the bombing of Heroshima.
But someone's gonna have to make a stand
Telling that sick and tired of being mocked.
Why am I the being pushed and shoved; why do I have to scream.
Is right for the bully to say you're nothing but a short stack nobody
Or your not perfect that you have a good personality or curves you threw a
Fastball but now I'm gonna swing and hit a home run for my team
I'm gonna put an end to this legendary streak it doesn't if 19 or 20
I'm gonna to 20 and I just to prove that you don't need a small kid or large kid
Just to stop the bullying and become a friend
Why am I the one

Maya Best

His Hands Like Coconut Shell
by Maya Best

His hands like coconut shell
With frostbitten fingers wrapped up in holey mittens.
His breath in front of him, disappearing in the winter breeze.
His aging face and wise old eyes.
The battered Styrofoam cup, held, jingling every so often,
In hopes that someone will spare just a little to find something to eat,
Or a new pair of shoes.
The shelter, overflowing with its crumbling walls,
And endless lines of people with nowhere else to go.
Children, cold and small,
Packed into the crowd, eager for a place to sleep, a single meal to eat.
Lost, confused, dreaming ...
Somewhere where jobs are abundant, where money spreads equally.
A place of second chances, starting afresh, mending his mistakes,
Living the life he never had.
Lights fading, stores closing, night approaching.
He clings to his jacket.
His cheeks scorched and stinging, the thump of his heart slowing, forgotten.
The cup stops jingling, the man stops breathing,
All is quiet now.

2nd Place

Jane Chen

The War of Countries
by Jane Chen

We are all created under the same sky.
Molded by the same pair of hands,
our breaths all saturated in the same clouds of air,
the feel of our palms indistinguishable to the blind man.
But the ignorant, shallow eyes of the seeing man
do not look past the shade of skin;
he is blinded by his sight
and he categorizes us neatly,
on the clearly labeled shelves of the mind.
Carved from ancient wood,
these shelves have forever separated us,
forcing us to subconsciously repeat
the deeply etched words on the lines of our faces.
Foolishly, we fight,
turning our noses up at our kin,
blinded by our differences.
Trapped by our ancestors' judgmental gazes, we try to resist:
Yet, we are all inevitably drawn
into the war of countries.

Bri Lewis

This year's overall winning entry
comes to us from a young lady in the ninth grade.
Bri Lewis offers an excellent case study in perspective,
and how the way people view the world around them
truly shows that beauty is, indeed, in the eye of the beholder.
It gives us great pleasure to present the work
of our 2013 Editor's Choice Award winner, Bri Lewis.

Editor's Choice Award

The Beholder
by Bri Lewis

Messily spray painted eyesores full of hate and vulgarity
Cover the decrepit buildings
Tiny, rundown houses are full of poor families
With never enough food on the table
And parents who are never home
Children play on fields now overrun with weeds and tall grass
Schools with barely any books and students who don't care enough to notice
Pathetic teachers who never really wanted this job, teach the few
Students who are naïve enough to think they've got a shot at escape
The stink of all the garbage on the streets
The worst part of town
Colorful depictions of social injustice displayed across large brick canvases
Small homes with big families and just enough love to go around
And parents who work extra hard around the clock
Children play on
Dedicated teachers who make up for a lack of materials with a love of the job
And instill a thirst for knowledge and a belief that anything is possible
In the students who will work at it
The smell of hard work and belief and hope
The best part of town
The same part of town

Division IV

Grades
10-12

Travis
by Shae Justice

Still to this day I have to wonder,
Where did you go?
Here I sit only five years old.
Outside I'm waiting for you to appear
Disappearing bird
Where did you go?
Colorful arrangement of smooth feathers,
Gone with no warning at all.

Life
by Amber Kneisler

Life
The thing we can't get back when we lose.
The ups and downs we might have
The things we can look at and be proud of.
Those dark times where all you want to do is be by yourself.
Those adventures you'll never forget
Things that are priceless.
The mistakes turned into lessons
Those pictures that will last forever
Those people that are always there for you.
Life

This Is Nature
by Jerry Runion

this is nature
but what is nature
nature is what
nature, is it life
The definition is what
Is it a natural area
to me nature is everything
what is nature to you
nature can be a forest
nature can be the woods
nature can be singing birds
but the question is
truly what is nature
that is for you to decide
and you to think about.

Darkness
by Adam Pieczynski

Darkness is the first real fear we ever have.
We have it till birth and for some it can last a lifetime
We fear the blackness, our lack of vision
Without our sight, even normal sounds will scare us.
With the terror darkness can bring it leaves me to believe
The blind are the bravest of us all

America
by Paige Ciarkowski

Home to many
and so not mini.
Love sure shows
watch out, nation grows.
People all around,
making many different sounds.
They are proud to be home
without a groan.
One nation always,
undivided by none.

Beach House
by McKenzie Steinke

Get away from you
Get away from all of the hurt you've caused
Get away from all the pain you've done
Just escape from all of it
And go to a place you'll never find me
Where there's tall glass windows, and golden wood flooring
And I'll leave the white glass doors wide open
So that the salty air can make it through them to my nose
I'll be sitting there on my bright white couch
That's when you'll try calling me and I'll pretend I never heard it
I'll just walk out of the room onto my deck where I'll just stand there
Looking out into the blue ocean
And having the sand sweep across my feet and tickle them
Ever so slightly
And I'll forget about you
And everything you've cause me to lose

Hidden Tears
by Stephanie Hite

Two blows to the face,
Smell of Vodka on his breath.
She tries to sob; she tries to hold it in.
Striking her dangling arms
For only three minutes,
But the scars last forever.
Hopeless questions, hurtful answers
"Keep this just between us" and "I love you".
Finally over for the day, she stumbles out of the door
Like crumpled Big Mac wrappers skittering across the pavement.
Feeling helpless and terrified;
She hobbles home, once again.

The Fool
by Joshua Chaney

I just earned a dollar hip-hip-hooray.
I am rich, I am "happy," I am successful, and live in the moment
and only for today.
I have land; I have money, and earthly possessions.
I invest my time into my goals and expectations.
I impress other people by the way I dress,
but I don't care what they think because I am the best
I am conceited, narcissistic, and self-centered.
"I" to me is the only thing that matters.
I enjoy my wealth, my power, my pride.
I've obtained it all through truth sprinkled with lies.
I can't handle authority, I make the rules.
I act like a dictator, the world's my footstool.
As my life has gone by and the years cycled through,
I've had everything I ever wanted. Now what is there left to do?
Life to me has become repetitive and boring.
Nothing, anymore to me, seems bright and alluring.
I am empty, hollow, alone my heart filled with pain.
I know there is more, but it's too late,
I missed it, I feel so ashamed.
All my pleasures in life were vanity,
Nihilism was my mind's front most mentality ... while living.
But I've passed through life's door.
How worthless and wasted I feel as I enter eternity.

America's True Meaning
by Erica Ataman

America means freedom.
It makes people proud.
As the sun rises over the blue water,
I am happy that I live free.
America the beautiful,
A country of greatness and wealth.
But it shows its true colors,
When you look in the slums.
Overridden with greed,
America has its troubles.
But even with all this going around,
It still carries on with patriotism.

Don't Ask, Don't Tell Is Dead
by Megan Scalzo

As a cloud of ash cleared the air I thought,
A thought that had loomed my mind for days,
When am I going to be discharged?
Discharged for being gay and wanting to serve in the military
The only things I could think about were my job in the military, and my boyfriend
I loved them both so much
I was frozen thinking the same thoughts
And questions that I wish I could tell my sergeant,
I'm mad, and deeply saddened that the military
Could discharge me for a simple thing like my sexual orientation
As the enemies fired back, men started to fall to the ground pierced with bullets
All the men in my unit knew my secret
And it did not change the bond we had together
No one cared when we were fighting shoulder to shoulder
I stood up and screamed, for all the homophobic people
That hated me and bullied in school
And I screamed for Don't Ask, Don't Tell to end
I closed my eyes wondering why I be fighting for rights
That I was not granted as a gay American
As I opened my eyes it gazed at me as if it knew something that I didn't
An AK-47 barrel was watching, waiting, and whispering for me
And after 18 long years, Don't Ask, Don't Tell is dead

A Flight of Fancy
by Nikoma Henkels

Does a bird get homesick
while on those long, yearly journeys around the world?
They travel miles and miles in a flick,
through the changing skies their bodies are hurled,
defying all ability of ours.
They navigate over land so vast,
we'd need a map or wonderful super powers
and even then, we'd never go as fast.
These little birds are driven by gut feeling.
They go on tradition and birdy religion.
Such devotion would leave us reeling,
stumbling around like drunk pigeons.
These birds have sacred spots,
far spread apart.
For a thing that flies into windows,
astounding is their memory of heart.

The Duplicitous Snow
by Katarina Hampton

A weathered piece of pottery
Marked of age with ebony hues,
Sepia tones compliment the scene of somber despair
For nothing from this little jar sprouts from the earth into clear view
The trampled weeds display no glimmer of life,
No will to survive or thrive in such a barren land, entwined with death's fiery might
The snow, a boastful white, a crisp chill, a gentle purity,
as delicate as pillows of meringue,
The small sugar crystals reflect the golden light,
directing our glance to its beautiful sight
Yet this delicate fluff strangles the green of its air,
Slaughters the wild beauty that once reigned
Replacing the life with its own presence,
While the green had little time to feel disdained
The fragility of life proves true in such a circumstance
Yet the emerald sprouts seem to return year after tiring year
Fighting for existence, never wavering,
eager to persevere and regain a stronghold in its domain
Snow, a fatal splendor, never can eradicate its existence,
as the green continues to return with vivid cheer.

Morning Leaves
by Lauren Ramer

The leaves sleep silently;
Their hues ranging from yellow to green to blue.
And in time they wake, fresh and clean,
Sprinkled with morning dew.
The thick broad surface
Of these leaves catches the stray raindrop
As it falls, landing on the
Smooth surface with an almost inaudible "plop."
Sitting among the flowers,
The modest leaves stay hidden
Until the passerby come near
And are drawn to them, unbidden.
The smooth, round balls of water
Are perched there so casually
As though they're some child's marbles
Set there until after tea.

Why Do You?
by Kari Ataman

Why are you pushing me to be this way?
Taking my mind and twisting it around.
Feeling like I'm being led astray,
From a place I always knew to be sound.
Why do you say the things you say?
To talk about me, to put me down.
As if I'm not good enough to stay,
Turning a once smile into a constant frown.
Why do you make me want an out?
To go to a place far away from here.
They say that Heaven is nice, I doubt
That anyone has seen a place so dear.
Why do you want me to leave so bad?
To get out of your life by ending my own.
Maybe if I left you wouldn't be so mad,
Ending a terror to which I have never known.
Is it pleasing you in any way?
To look at me and see me bleed.
I hope you're happy; you got your way,
Death shall bring the peace I need.

It's Up To You
by Renee Wolosion

Everyday a new child is born
From them on, they are made to soar
Soar to wherever they want to go
Soar at any speed, fast or slow
In this land, where we are all free
We are taught to always believe
Believe in whatever we want
Believe, and never stop
The sky is a big mystery
It holds many things we never see
We don't see what the clouds might bring
We don't hear what the wind might sing
Yes the sky is a mystery
But so is the land of the free
Nothing is meant to be
We can choose what we see
Nothing is meant to be.

Christmas Sauna
by Ingrid Flaspohler

It was a warm winter day
My brother carried the saw
We look for a tree of just the right size, shape, and height
Then we see what we think is the one
The perfect Christmas tree
I cut through it halfway and my brother finishes the cut
We load the tree in the back of the truck
My brother, mother, father, and me
We travel to our cottage on Lake Superior
My father starts the sauna fire
As it heats we walk down the beach
The frog pond is frozen over
In our eyes it is an ice rink
Then the sauna is ready
We change into our swimsuits
Stepping into the heat the smell of cedar reaches my nose
The floor is cold but the air is warm
A warm room in the middle of winter
A Christmas sauna

Diving Legion
by Armani Gregory

Unreached commitment
Unleashes a relentless road
Eroding in concrete cement souls
Exploding into deceased remains
Molding to pieces of strange lanes
The danger will condense
For plainer sensible recognition
Unexplainable superstition
Outreached lies
Dies in reason
Through a seasoned spice
"Diving Legion"
An array of decayed dedication
Sincere irritation
Compose from my alliteration
Conceives published imitation of insanity
The sanity Satan grinds
Then finds forms of calamity
Which unstrengthens me?

Waiting
by Hunter Hoogewind

I'll never stop liking you,
I just won't always show it,
Waiting.
I'll never stop talking to you,
I just won't always listen,
Waiting for you to hear me.
I'll never stop caring about you,
I just won't always be there for you to lean on,
Waiting for you in return.
I'll never stop crying about you,
I just don't let you see me cry,
Waiting for you to care.
I'll never stop thinking about what could have been,
I just won't let it run my life,
Because waiting for you is disappointing.
If it takes this long,
It was never meant to be,
Waiting.

Usually, Not Unusual, a Very Unusual Poem
by Daniel Henderson

Conforming to the normal, is very normal
Independent thinking is independent living
Those who follow are living someone's life
Majority live a lie
Walk through the world and characterize fashion trends
The few that dress unusual are unusual
The unusual are usually successful
But then again, what is success to an unusual person
Success and happiness are synonyms
But does that mean you have to be happy to find success
Some may find a way to be successfully happy
You could also be successful in conforming
This is the time where you're pondering conformity
Don't be worried, you will be successful

Luna
by Lauren Livengood

The moon is the dreamer, the sun is the dream.
She caresses the world with her midnight gleam.
As long as she shines, I know inside,
that the world, in the end, will turn out right.
If the dark is real and the light the mirage,
is it really you here or just your visage?
In the blossoms of hearts and vastness of heads,
the moon allows for such beautiful treks.
Across the sea, across the sky,
you can steal the wind and learn to fly.
It's mourning again, and alas what a shame,
it's morning light that's to blame
for stealing my true eyes away.
With all the war and the hate,
I can't hardly wait
until the night prevails once more.
To live in the smog and the noise and the glare,
that the night can't be longer it just isn't fair
So I can be under the moon and the stars that shine,
Where I can just drift away, and the magic is mine.

Outdoor Shoots
by Aubrey Zackal

The lake is solid
Frozen to the sand
Hear it expanding through the night
Hockey players here and there
The sound of sticks hitting the lake
The shout of screams when there is a goal
The winds will just whisper
Your ears will freeze
Even with your hat and helmet on
To watch the trees blow with the wind
To watch the puck slide far onto the ice
The lake expands just one more time
With cracking through the night
This is hockey at its best
On Lake Superior one late night

My Angel
by Stephanie Simon

The second that I heard your first cry,
I was so happy and I knew that we would have a great life together,
They had to take you to be examined right after you were born,
You arrived a little early but I didn't think much of it,
One minute everything was perfect and the next everything fell apart,
When the doctor came in and gave me news my heart shattered
How could this happen? Did I do something wrong?
When I heard your little heart beat for the first time I feel in love with you instantly,
You were loved from the second that you were created
and you will always be loved,
No matter what you will always be with me,
You are my Angel watching over me from above
The doctor told me how sorry he was but there was nothing that he could do,
You were gone and you are never coming back,
One minute you were healthy, kicking your little feet around,
the next you weren't breathing,
Was there something that I could have done to keep that from happening?
In the little life that you had you brought so much happiness,
I never got to hold you but you were so beautiful and so perfect
How can I possibly say goodbye when I never even got to say hello?
You are my Angel watching over me from above

English Poems
by Brendan Alkevicius

What if I didn't type these poems,
I might just fail this class.
What if I failed this class,
I might not graduate.
What if I didn't graduate,
I might never get a good job.
Wouldn't that just be a failure?

Perseverance
by Kelli Jackson

As you wait and ponder what is on your mind
You wonder when it will be your time to shine
With no time to wait and wonder
The thoughts you ponder start to flounder
Making your dreams come true is going to need some helpful clues
Giving up is like a tattoo that you can never remove
Or not having the chance to improve
Just believe in yourself
That is all you need to do
To become your best in this faithful quest ...
We call our dreams

The Hunters
by Jordan Herrmann

You see them come; you try and hide
But you hear them whisper, see the hunt in their eyes.
You take off running; no place is safe
You hear them coming, feel the chase.
They prey on your faults, every one
Hunters they are– these hungry ones.
They taste your fear, every drop
Abandon your pride– just don't stop.
You've got a chance; your pack is near.
Faster, faster– they're almost here
There's one more hall; they see you come
Breathe, breathe– you have won
But the hunters remain–
Always watching,
Always waiting,
And always ready to pounce.

Emotionless
by Ashley Chauvin

Stomped
in distraught rage
raising
his voice
every two words
screaming
yelling
in terror
His rage
continued on
never ending
back and forth
increasing volume
screamed
exasperated
I just sat
terrified
motionless
emotionless

Joy Is a Luminous Moon
by Cailin Klick

Vanishing behind the clouds
Unaware of its power
Permanently there
Yet not always seen
Illuminating the surrounding sky
All embrace the radiance
Welcoming the infamous smile
Mimicking the face they perceive
Splendor is found from within
Waiting for the adequate moment
It glistens through the skin
Enduring the prolonged day
Obscure unless in mind
It goes without acknowledgement
Foreseen from within a dream
Existence is dull without inner shine

Revelation
by Meg Notoriano

The most mysterious things
Appear dull and fearful,
My violent, bright hues
Hidden from people.
What you don't know
Is what you can't see,
An untamable muse,
Burning in me.
No words could suffice
Or capture the thoughts,
That hide in my head
Escaping your scoffs.
My eager heart
Stains all who breathe,
Tainting you slowly
Never wanting to leave.
Humbled by freedom
No longer concealed,
I pattern you freely,
True colors revealed.

Beauty
by Mariah Schepak

Society has an addiction to perfection
Perfect bodies, perfect skin, perfect hair, perfect smile
People think that only perfection is beautiful
And yet, there is no such thing as perfection
Teenage girls- young women- starve themselves to be thinner,
Cover skin blemishes with makeup
Waste money on new clothes every season
Young girls are beginning to view themselves as fat when they look in the mirror
Not knowing how thin they actually are
Not knowing that beauty is imperfection
That beauty is in the curve of a belly
The birthmark that lies on one cheek
The one strand of hair that won't stay in place
The crookedness of a smile
That beauty lies in the girl who embraces her body
Who loves herself for how she was made, for who she is
Because beauty comes from love, and if people love themselves
Then they will always be beautiful
Even if they aren't perfect

The Kiss
by Dakota Brown

Where the hills dip
lies a little lake,
with winds that nip
the gentle wake.
That is where
I will take you;
to a hidden lair
and kiss you anew.
On the blue water
or its grassy shore.
In Summer's mutter
of Winter's roar.
At the little lake,
a kiss I will take.

On His Death
by Amanda Daly

My Grandpa was a memorable man
So upsetting he had to die
I was just six, when I was told he was gone
For ten years of my life
I have been in a battle as to why he died
I remember me on his lap
Signing me sweet stories of life in our own language
My Grandpa was a gift
For who will see no gift in a Grandpa?
Though I never knew him to the fullest
I knew I had a Grandpa
His death has brought me pain
To see me without a grandpa
A destiny not to be wasted
I feel I am at rest
Although Grandpa is gone
Sadness still dwells as of late
My life is like a rose
Laid in the midst of thorns, still blossoming
For when a Grandpa is lost, A Grandpa is surely found.

Ode To Heroes
by Dakota Kipper

The sun will rise for us this day,
So gentle in its light.
And though the dead will fade away,
We never will lose sight.
So gentle in its light,
The sun shall set on all the gods made.
As the world falls into night,
We stand ready with shield and blade.
The sun shall set on all the gods made
While blood spills upon the field.
We stand ready with shield and blade.
The will of the gods we still wield.
While blood spills upon the field,
And though the dead will fade away,
The will of the gods we still wield.
The sun will rise for us this day.

Untitled
by Kevin Bacon

What's the use?
Of what can I expect?
If anything?
Anything at all?
I can't.
For conviction, I do not feel.
Truth, I do not want it to be.
My rain may not be heard;
I still wish for you to know.
I care.
Irrevocably.
I won't ever not;
What may appear to be faulty,
will be held
by my gaze–
But into my eyes of the rose,
must you choose to wander,
shall lie the seed.
For which will ignite
as heat against romaine.

Planting the Seed
by Genna Kyle

You planted the seed,
A seed of pure desire.
Sprouting roots of sickness
Extending thirsty power
Darkness, watering all.
Planted deep,
Near the fiery pit of pain
Warming its frosted leaves.
Growing,
Reaching the sky
Touching tips of night
Darkness, its gardener.
Dips fertilizer in roots
Encourages growth
Desire, running up and down its stem.
No longer a seed,
But a plant of misery
That you breathed life into
Urging the darkness to grow.

TwoNineSevenSeven: Casualties of Nine-Eleven
by Georgia Gregoricka

When disaster struck on that September day,
Children, adults, elders, didn't know how to respond.
The Silence took over America.
People scattered and ran when the dust and rubble appeared;
When realization kicked in, citizens took their place,
And the brave took charge.
Volunteers, firefighters, and police, rushed inside the burning building.
Even though they tried hard to save innocent lives,
Some carried out the deceased. Although scared, they still proceeded.
Televisions were turned on in every household,
And the tears ran on, uncontrolled.
Melancholy took over.
The towers no longer stood tall in New York City,
And yet there is still that empty feel.
Now the remembrance casts our hearts into deep despair.
Sadness and confusion is in every soul when nine-eleven is recalled,
Almost like an optical illusion, the terrorist attack,
Still boggles our minds.
The brave volunteers and the losses will forever be, always in our hearts.
May they rest in heaven. The day of nine-eleven will always be remembered.

Reflected Glass
by Faith Briggs

I look into the mirror,
into a plane of reflected glass.
I see a face I don't recognize,
features blurred behind a mask.
Blue eyes that are like windows,
a peek into the soul.
But the windows are locked,
and the fire has grown cold.

To You My Friend
by Stuart Nielsen

It's funny how a melody sounds like a memory
Till this day I still remember the times it used to be
Just you and me
We were wild and free
Wind in our hair and at our feet
Without a doubt we faced defeat
Tattoos and black eyes
Dark nights and gray skies
To the day we meet again
Just you and me
like old friends

In the Walls of the Alamo
by Kate Noorman

Etched into the wall are the voices of the dead.
I run my prints across it to feel each groove.
I can tell the differences - what part of the letter took more force to inscribe.
I can feel the frustration - ridden anger that fueled the hands of a man
who felt so deeply betrayed by his fellow men.
I can feel the shattered heart of a child
who wished to be in the arms of his mother
who so lovingly welcomed heaven's gates.
In the walls of the Alamo, I can feel the pain.
I press it into my hand like jagged thorns,
hoping that a shred of their suffering and sorrow would make a change in me,
so that their tragedy wouldn't have been for nothing.

Home
by Kaitlyn Sterling

Having a place
One can call sanctuary.
Molding a haven,
Escaping reality.

Little Sister
by Aisha Ehrhart

Oh, little sister of mine
How I love you so
Your smile lights up my room
Lovingly, you skip away
Knowing you'll be back to smile another day
By the way, I don't know what I would do without you
Oh, little sister of mine
How I love you so

The Oceans Waves
by Victoria Pekarek

The waves of the water splash up against my feet
Bring the sand between my toes
And the rocks piercing my shins
The laughter of when you run into the waves
The sea splashing your bare belly up to the tip of your chin
You take the first plunge
Feeling the rush of the chill run up and down your body
You take the second plunge
But the waves increase their strength
Feeling the waves bringing you down
Farther than you would like
The waves take a punch into your feet
Knocking them out from under you
They take the next punch in your stomach
Knocking the breath out of you
Your eyes pop open
You see the whirlpool above you but it is only getting more distant from you
You reach your hand up as if it will grab your hand
And pull you towards air but you only sink deep
Until the ocean blue turns to dark blue and the dark blue turns to black

I Want You
by Cortez Jordan

I want to write a Book,
Publish it, then classify it as science fiction
Because the way you make me feel inside just can't be real
Have every paragraph be a testimony of my love for you
Every chapter will be a handbook
for every guy that came before me and failed
Seems that every time I write about Love … my pencil breaks,
Just to show that it's going to take a little more work than before
But you're worth it
I could write a million books
I could read a thousand stories
I could even read the dictionary for the rest of my life
And I would still never find one word to describe how much you mean to me
But for the purpose of this poem I have 3,
That I'll promise forever if you Love me
This poem is getting too long so I must be through,
I will end it with an I Want You

A Wooded Walk
by Hannah Gundlach

As one walks along a wooded path
early on a spring morning.
They will find the moss and flowers
covered in golden, shimmering dew drops
the diamonds of the forest.
They will smell the bittersweet pine trees
towering, their scraggly limbs searching the sky for the sun.
They will hear the wistful songs of the birds,
calling to a lover, or perhaps the sky itself,
in the hope of something calling back.
They might find their troubles of the past
crumbling like dry, crimson colored, autumn leaves,
their worries dissolving, being absorbed by good thoughts
like the dewdrops in the moss.
They might discover their memories rushing past
as fast as the cars on the freeway.
Both good and bad, leaving a nostalgic air about them for the moment.
And as one walks along a wooded path
early on a spring morning.
They may find that their outlook on life
has been changed for the better.

Bare Nirvana
by Jessica Lewis

Wind caresses my face and neck, hair flowing gently behind my shoulders.
Hot sun blazes across the thin veils of my eyelids,
Stinging in a pleasant, embracing way.
Shuddering, I absorb the warmth; it seeps into the pores of my skin
And brings life to the shattered glass statue I had become.
It wasn't always like this; I never used to have to escape my own skin.
I used to love who I am—was. I used to laugh at myself and my mistakes.
Used to. But now–now I shed my acrimonious prison for a place
Where my heart can soar and leap.
Here I can run and spin and dive, here I can sprout new legs,
Or take off into the sky to discover a world previously only fantasized.
Here I am free. Truly free, without the bars and wires and traps set out before,
That were invisible only to the eyes.
I am no longer that lone wanderer, stranger not only unto the world,
But unto myself as well.
Nay–I do not cry dew upon the grass, but kiss open the lids of morning.
The prison gates have been stripped away; I am here. Free in America.

Remember When?
by Bailey Gulch

Remember when?
Remember when it was just the two of us?
Remember when every photo I owned had you in it?
Remember when we would spend all summer together?
Remember when we would complain about being apart?
Remember when we would partner up for every project?
Remember when we would run through the sprinklers together?
Remember when life was perfect?
Remember when we grew up?
Remember when we started high school and I never got to see you?
Remember when you chose band and I chose choir?
Remember when you got a boyfriend?
Remember when you told me to go away so you could be with him alone?
Remember when I fell head over heels for a boy?
Remember when you told me to stop acting like he was mine?
Remember when you canceled your plans with me to be with him?
Remember when you left me in the dust crying?
Remember when reality came crashing down on me?
Remember when I realized it wasn't just the two of us anymore?
Do you even remember when it was just the two of us?
Do you?

The Beauty of Growth
by Elizabeth Bowen

The seed was sown
The earth was expectant
Spring for the rose came
Without a warning
The love needed for growth became manifest
It came with the purest of wills, a most gracious intention
Quite unexpectedly, the rose then grew
She grew with the realization that this pain was very new.
As she was forced out of the dark, her young heart trembled
The love slowly, softly became undeniable
Each velvet petal unfolded, each bit of her core revealed
She reveled in the sunlight (the joy of being known)
Fear was washed by truth
Her soul was cleansed by transparency
The love so freely given
Was kissed by a Southern Wind

At Least I Have the Memories
by Danelle Leppek

Looking at the casket as it sits there open wide
I feel like I'm alone even though my family is by my side.
This day was just the worst,
Feeling like my heart was going to burst.
I needed her comfort on this dark lonely day.
There was only one thing left to say
At least I have the memories.
She was the best and she always knew,
she was always there to watch me as I grew.
I needed her love and she showed she cared,
I always loved her curly hair.
I loved her laughter when we played,
Because of this I have to say
At least I have the memories.
When I was little and I cried
she was an angel in my eyes,
And still today this holds true.
When I look up to heaven and say Grandma I love you.
There's one last thing I'd like to say,
Thank you for the memories.

A Poem Within My Mind
by Heather Baker

I don't know, I just don't know,
What am I supposed to write,
What should I write is the actual question,
A poem with a soul,
A rhythmic ring and art-like structure,
Is uncommon by my hand for I am no poet,
The poem I reach is out of reach,
Many perfect poems swim inside my head,
All beautiful and elegant for the paper,
But they scatter once a pen is grasped by my hand,
And that is just it,
They all scatter,
Constantly moving,
Changing,
Rearranging continuously,
No longer detectable in my mind,
Will I ever find that perfect poem?

My Little Magic Box
by Beth Schwab

When I open my little magic box,
I am welcomed into a world
Of yellowing paper and black ink.
In the world of my imagination,
I soar on the backs of dragons;
Fight in epic battles beside my king.
I wield a sword and shoot a bow,
I pitch knives at thieves,
And run about risking my life
For my sister and mother.
In this world of beautiful words,
I gallivant in a field with my lover,
I dance at a ball in the arms of my prince.
I sing a lullaby
To the tune of an old music box.
I weep for a friend
That has passed away from me
And for the love that I will never have.
But it all comes to an end,
When I close my little magic box.

Rope Burns
by Kim Baetz

You're stiller than you should be,
you do not make a sound.
Your voice cried out for someone,
but no one was around.
So you did something drastic,
you climbed into the air,
but instead of touching down again,
you're still just hanging there.

Worries
by Emily Morlan

You pick up a stone
You throw it so far
The troubles you have
Are gone and withdrawn
The stone hits the ground
You feel light, so free
You look for the landing
It hits, cracks, and blasts.
You see pieces sparkle
Diamonds so swell
The bad things you had
Aren't bad after all

Hand In Hand
by Michaela Burton

Good and bad come hand in hand
one wears a flamboyant suit of vibrant colors
catching the eye of all
every move he makes is duly noted and observed
he is the star of his own show
and society pays to attend
the other wears a simple outfit
and blends in with a crowd
going undetected for all he does
and yet
they walk together
hand in hand

Wiggle Worm
by Molly Sprague-Rice

Yapping all around,
running in circles.
Wonderment shown in
his eyes. The first
time being outside
is the greatest.
Trying to wiggle under
the fence to escape is
a great feat. You have
only 3 legs and you are
too dark to go noticed.
Let's just be leashed
and go on a walk instead.

Love of a Nation
by Cassandra Davis

Love is like a cool summer breeze enveloping your willing heart,
caressing the very essence of your soul.
Love is taking hold of your life, welcoming in a burst of pure content.
Like a Blue Jay's soft song and like a dove's tranquil chirp;
Love soars on the wings of America's great eagles
and glides over the exquisite purple mountains of majesty.
Gripping the firm soil of our patriots who fought and died for one nation,
leaving a trail of history forged in and by Love,
creating friendship between the free and forever equal races of humanity.
Love glistens in the multicolored lights that dance in the northern sky.
Love encourages the strong like a burst of wind encouraging the trees.
The land of the brave will push forward like Freedom Riders;
bring support to our standing forces and provide safety for every youth
PROUD to be an American.
Love will always dare us to discover and explore,
never commanding to stray in fear.
We will never relinquish our rights, we will stand tall against all fights.
Love is what binds us with every morsel of our being,
filling us until we overflow with passion.
It's what we crave at night when the moon whispers its goodnight,
and during the day when the sun greets us with blazing luminance.
Love is like a cool summer breeze enveloping your willing heart,
caressing the very essence of your soul, telling you to come home.

Mysteries Ahead
by Ashley Fultz

The emptiness of the beautiful forest
Where no one knows what may lie ahead.
What creatures or mysteries await,
We just have to imagine and wonder instead.
Upon the trees of different sizes,
Are leaves of bright and fiery gold.
As I notice all of the beautiful scenery,
I imagine all of the stories to be told.
Stories about things no one can see
That are masked by the wonderful view,
Until we enter the unknown
Or stop and think about something fresh and new.
I watch in amazement as I walk
At how the trees sit so still as day moves to night.
I don't know what draws me back here,
But something about it feels so right.

Winter's War
by Theresa Payne

Frigid winds whimper
Eyes of the sky crying snow
Soft and subtle flakes drift
Frosted windows with peering light
Lamps on the sidewalks illuminating the way
Steps untraceable with benches dampened
Clouds gathered closely
The peaking sun's rays are broke
Chilling air biting everything in sight
Swirls retreated to hollow trees
Nothing, but empty streets
Her skin blushed
Fingers numb
Feet giving into the ground
Eyes glazed with exhaustion
Hair matted within a hat
Having no sense of direction
Ice beneath the snow
Catching her feet
Lying all alone

Elly's Cry
by Brooklynn Ketterman

Everywhere I go the cries, they follow,
Screaming and crying the same agonizing whimpering,
Elly, her screams come so helpless, so faint,
Dead of night the cries linger, cold and alone,
As though they haunt me,
So helpless, she lay cold as ice,
Breaking towards new beginnings,
Suddenly everything is silent,
For the moment there is peace,
Hell seems to break through now,
The screams even louder,
Cries of her poor soul,
Shattering the silence like broken glass,
She has been gone away years ago,
Yet her cries still linger,
Forever I am haunted by the death of a baby's cry,
Sorrowful screaming,
Yet no one knows why.

Power of the Horizon
by Anna Mahalak

There comes a time where one must make a decision
To sink, or swim; to look back, or fight on
As I look forward on this bridge I realize
That my decision is coming as quickly as the approaching of dawn
I look around at the horizon ahead
At the indigo lake and the shades of coral and yellow quartet
In my head I imagine the end of this path
While I bask in the beauty and warmth of this sunset
Suddenly the view overtakes my mood
And everything feels as if it will be okay
It is as though the sun is guiding me
And even though I felt lost before, I now know my way
Before I went through life not appreciating its wonder
I walked around with my head down under a cloud of doom
Everything was strictly business with no magic or pizzazz
Now because of this simple wondrous sight my imagination can bloom

Survival of the Fittest
by Lauren Bukowski

Sitting in my nice, warm house
On a blustery, cold winter day
I watch and wait and wonder
When will a squirrel come my way?
After minutes of eagerly waiting
For some lively nature to make a show,
I see a squirrel the color of coal
Eating the seeds that fell below.
I see the little squirrel standing so lonely
Like a girl quietly waiting in an empty café,
Or a fisherman in his shanty
On the ever so frozen bay.
However, a squirrel must do what a squirrel must do.
Eating is first priority on his little to-do list.
No friends, no family, only food on his mind;
It's something that we call "survival of the fittest".

Growing Up
by Jazmine Gaston

We weren't supposed to be here.
It wasn't allowed.
It's too far away for our moms to see
But high enough to touch a cloud.
The air was thick and clingy-
Kind of like my grandma's sweater.
But in here, we were free and cool.
It made us feel better.
The sun crept in around us
While the wind let out a shout
With each rustling of the branch,
They plotted to reveal our secret hideout.
Don't think we're bad.
We just wanted to go exploring.
Every day we'd get higher and higher.
Never will this get boring.
Plus we promised to see our new friends
Up there on the seventh twig.
They were small and curious, just like us
Straining their necks to understand a world so big.

Shine Through
by Sarah Hirschmann

There are two parts of nature
There is only one people want to see
There is the photographed and the ignored
Even when it comes to me.
There are pretty trees
With the sun shining through
What is it like behind the picture?
You haven't got a clue.
It is the same for life
There is the shared and the covered.
The part people want to hear
And the part they barely muttered.
Life is nature.
We are all living things
So be yourself
And see what life brings.

Words Left Unspoken
by Kiana Thomas

The forest's face forgotten
Beauteous branches left broken
I hear welcoming whispers
I listen to words left unspoken
I inhale the aroma around arrogantly
I stay starved of the natural world
Never braver standing secluded
My head sat hanging, my neck curled
The wailing waters waving farewell
Sun shows shining through the leaves
I turn to take a last peek
The wind blows, binds, and breathes
I never want to forget again
Stay forever isolated from the rest
Responsibilities reduced to nothing
I just listen to the noise fest
How can I leave behind such beauty?
I have no choice
The darkness pulls me farther away
My last breath is one of rejoice

Rose
by Alexandra Warminski

What if we were forever?
And our lives were so much more
Than a weeping, wilting, white little rose
Lying on the earthy floor
What if we had meaning?
Beginning at birth and ending in death
Working toward goodness, love, and purity
With our every waking breathe
What if we love one another?
Unconditionally and without question
To care, to comfort, to counsel
Hate would never be a suggestion
What if we learned to live more?
More fully than a rose
Whose only purpose in this world
Is for beauty that quickly goes

As Fire Does Fall
by Leo Schuster

Descending from the sky in their majestic grace
Falling fast, splicing the air as they go
Unknowing of their terrible, fiery embrace
They looked upon the world, what a beautiful place
Passing through the air, going with its unending flow
Descending from the sky in their majestic grace
The beautiful lights, the city below, how they wished to touch base
Growing ever closer, able for the grand architecture to show
Unknowing of their terrible, fiery embrace
The beauty!, The mastery!, Adoring as they fell through space
They gazed at the streets and alleys below
Descending from the sky in their majestic grace
"No!, Why must we destroy this city's beautiful face!"
Too late, hitting the ground, enshrouding the city in its terrifying glow
Unknowing of their terrible, fiery embrace
How could they have known the terrible purpose of their race?
Cursing their lives as they raised the city low
Descending from the sky in their majestic grace
Unknowing of their terrible, fiery embrace

Unspoken
by Mary Gatto

I saunter to the tree, admiring its entanglement,
mazed in a contorted barbed snag,
every point extended to meet the somber horizon.
Mimicking hands grasp the unspoken celestial sphere
displaced among the piercing vines.
I ponder how it never ceases to plunder any sparrow's breast.
The thorns, insulting to a human's touch,
So entrapping yet so harmless,
Captivating, thus trustworthy to my youthful mentality.
I am but a stranger to nature's enduring haze,
Yet, I acquire my nobility by its omniscient ways.

At the Airport Near the Graveyard
by Nayereh Doosti

In my hometown, there's an airport near the memorial park
At the airport near the memorial park,
it's hard to let your last image have a smile on
At the airport near the memorial park,
it's hard to see your mom's tears behind her glasses,
At the airport near the memorial park,
it's hard to see your dad's teardrops sliding down those sun burnt cheeks
At the airport near the memorial park, it's hard, everything gets hard
You swallow your tears, lock them up in your throat,
and keep them for your long flight
Then it gets hard to breathe, you try to calm everyone down,
you try to make them laugh
You do anything to hide your tears. You try to act like nothing is going to change.
At the airport near the memorial park,
it's hard to agree with your friends when they say
you're lucky that you're going to America, this "dream land".
It's hard ...
At the airport near the memorial park,
you feel the pain you've felt many times before
At the airport near the memorial park,
you can't remember how many people you lost
All is left is you, the pain, and an airport near a memorial park,
At the airport near the memorial park, it's your turn ...
At the airport near the memorial park there's a graveyard
A graveyard as vast as my hometown
A graveyard
As broad as my memories ...

L'amour En Froid
by Aubrey Anderson

Struggling for the deep warmth,
We lay, side to side.
Trapped by the
Cold, drafting, unspeakable
forces, that prey
on everything near.
Clutching each other,
we sigh, in unison
in the unmitigated presence
that keeps coming,
going on and on and on
Until with a loud shriek,
burst we up
"Carpe diem!" cried we, together
so, together, we seize the day
Ignoring the forces
which lingered still
in that hard, long day

In the Shadows of a Smile
by Rylie Store

If you look in her eyes, deeper than before,
Past the colors and lashes, you'll unlock a door.
A door to her secrets, sadness, and fears,
To a girl who'd never before shed a tear.
Her screams so loud, they dissolve to mute.
Her body trembles as she becomes a pathetic brute.
The questions people asked about her pale scarred wrists,
She'd only laugh, and lie about her decaying wits.
Her lies were masked by a fake awkward smile,
And her body so empty for too long of a while.
The blade slices one pore at a time,
As she follows the pattern of her life's new rhyme.
The blood trickles like freshly spilt paint,
She swallows hard so she doesn't faint.
She lies her head down on her pillow to rest,
And clutches hard for the heart beneath her breast.
She blinks her last blink and cries her last cry,
Another young girl, is about to die.
Her mother no idea and her father no clue,
And the girl no longer trapped like glue.

Leaf
by Mason Miller

Floating through the air,
Landing softly on the ground,
Leaves fall from the tree.

To Fly
by Lilli Larson

I sit here quietly, amongst the vines,
Marveling at the passing time.
Listening intently to the willow rhyme,
Talking to the spirit, Divine.
With the stream speaking in babbles,
My mind takes a swim,
Past memories and thoughts I paddle,
I twirl around as if on a whim.
With this pain in my core,
I cannot bear it for a moment more.
I will not lead this life with a script of bore.
We were created with the gift to explore.
My mind breaks free from the lines that confine me,
And with this new strength I soar high
To places where only God will find me.
Now I know what it is to fly.

Caring Is a Journey
by George Ethan Duffield

A long way from home
Lots of road before me
Thoughts of stopping arise
Driving is therapy
Speed is a cure
Distance covered makes me nervous
Engine is reality
The windshield is the future
The rear-view is the past
Feelings get in the way
People become puzzles
Attempting to forget
Memories battle back
Warfare is my brain
Caring is a journey

Blemished Beauty
by Hayley Durham

Sliver is plain
Like the moon,
Blemished, yet beautiful
Beyond words,
Plain and beautiful,
Like I.

River
by Madison Labyak

I walked on down to the river today,
To feel the peace,
To get away.
As I walked I looked down,
To see a face staring back at me.
She looked familiar,
I knew her face,
But who was she?
To the right,
And to the left,
She followed my every move.
She was my new best friend.
Can't you see.
She was a double.
A double of me.

Dreary Day
by Julia Weller

Oh what a dreary day.
The sun won't shine, the birds refuse to chirp, and everyone has a frown.
Oh what a dreary day.
The sky is gray, the wind keeps rolling by, and the rain has started to come.
Oh what a dreary day.
The hours drag on and the homework is piled high.
Oh what a happy day it will be when summer is here!
The colors will be bright and the sun will extend its rays.
Oh what a happy day it will be when summer is here!
The beach sand warm, the ocean water cool and refreshing, and the sunglasses on.
Oh what a happy day it will be when summer is here!
The grill turned on, the campfire blazing, and the school is empty.
You will know when summer is here because everyone will be glad and smiling.

Attack Cat
by Rachel Hackett

Fat cat's paws
Falling, flaky snow
Fierce yellow eyes
Fighting to catch the crow, kitty, no!
Eager jaws
Pressed against the window
Valiantly he tries
To get out in the snow.
Sharp claws
Spotted sparrow
Small size
Silly kitty, you can't go!
But the cat has his flaws
He pounced too low:
Saying his good byes
To the crow.

Let Me Live
by Chelsey Kuikstra

Let me live again
Let me dream of how things were
Let life be my grass I walk on
Looking for a place to stay free
I am a young girl, clinging onto my hope
Torn in two by hands of endless hurt
Of beating, bruised, tormented, and confused
Of pampered to fix! Of pampered to a way of being sorry!
Of yelling from you! Of taking the pain!
Of an act of love seen ever so not real
Slapped back for being stupid because you too were there
Yet won't admit that you did this to me
I am a young girl who lives in hell
Visual tears tell me nothing more than pain.
Yet I'm the one to blame for this
In the lifeless world where I was still me
Who dreamt a dream so wrong, so long, so true
That even if it was right
In every light and window, in every corner of my room
That's made me stronger than any man

Forever Free
by Katlyn Wheeler

"Take my hand and come with me.
You can escape this place and be set free,"
The tall soldier pleaded with fearful eyes.
Bombs exploded near and far.
The curly-haired, blue-eyed girl never made it out.
"Take my hand and come with me.
You can escape this place and be set free,"
An angel whispered, reaching for the little girl.
Seeing Mommy and Daddy again, she agreed.
"Take my hand, sir. Stand with me.
You can escape this pain; You set me free,"
The blue-eyed girl sung to the soldier.
Tears slid down his smiling face.
"She is free, I am free,"
He whispered in August, 1945.
"Her battle is over, this war is ending.
She is free, I am free.
Forever engraved in memory."

Yellow
by Samantha Reilly

Yellow rain cascades over the wealthy crowd,
Over golf courses, porches, and country clubs alike.
While the poor man outside the cloud,
Rides his bike.
Yellow cars, yellow daisies,
The yellow rain could make a sane man crazy.
Not one remains unaffected by
That great yellow cloud in the sky.
The man with the bike sees another, in the center of the rain,
He is intrigued by the man.
He throws great parties but his only companion remains
That constant, eerie, green light that never wanes.
That yellow rain fills the pool
Where a man's path is sure to end.
He does not go like a fool,
But a man with only one friend.
There's nothing to gain from staying near the cloud,
So the man pedals out West with a bellow.
Where the rain is clear and loud
But the fields are still yellow.

Once Upon a Time
by Emily Wilson

Once the rose was red
Now wilted and dead
And alone on the ground.
What was it for
Once upon a time?
Maybe once it was for
A love, Gone.
Maybe once it was for
A funeral, Died.
Maybe once it was for
A mother, Forgotten.
Maybe once it was for
A wife, Betrayed.
Maybe once it was for
A child, Killed.
Although never the same
The story died, With the rose.
We may never know,
The story of What was
Once upon a time.

Endless Maze
by Brad Fauteux

I'm still trying to escape this maze.
The confusion running 'round my brain,
And I'm hoping we can end this phase.
Trying to escape your sinister gaze,
For it seems to have become my bane.
I'm still trying to escape this maze.
I've become obsessed with your strange ways,
Feels like I'm falling down an endless drain,
And I'm hoping that we can end this phase.
Standing here inside the strangest haze,
I don't know how much more I can sustain.
I'm still trying to escape this maze.
Wondering why I'm suffering this daze,
For it seems to be caused by your endless reign,
And I'm hoping that we can end this phase.
I've become obsessed in your strange ways,
They seem to cause me much pain.
I'm still trying to escape this maze,
And I'm hoping that we can end this phase.

Let Me Sleep On It
by Benjamin Li

O sleep, O sleep, as soft as leaping lambs.
So sweet to slip in, but trouble to wake.
To you, I ask a question easy as cake:
Are you compassion; or are you a scam?
Because without your gift, no doubt I can
Discover time to finish now, with headache
Tomorrow disappeared– instead, a break!
But why art thou so comfortable, like yam?
'Tis not a question of try or not to try.
While some see sleep necessity, I see
That sleep's serenity. Today to fly,
And manage time, then rest, and sleep like the sea.
Because to sleep becomes not time wasting by.
To sleep is to live; for we love all we see.

4th and Long
by Joseph Smith

It's that time, it's that quarter of the game,
When you have to decide whether to lose or journey to fame.
All that work after school, and work after hours
Comes down to this moment, separating men from cowards.
One more play says your coach, and one more presentation says your boss.
You've worked so hard to be this far, and you don't want to take a loss.
And now you have a decision, to rise above or should you fall.
Are you going to write that last paper, or throw that last ball.
You know it will hurt, and be very long and hard.
But you dig deep down inside and pull out one last card.
The clock is ticking, time is starting to run out,
There is so much pressure that you just might stop and shout.
But there's no time for that, you can rest when you are done.
For when you finish this task, then you can have some fun.
So you start typing away on your computer,
and getting ready for one last play.
Your mind is set and determined, so losing there's no way.
Hike! You get the ball and run with all your might.
You may begin, says your boss, as you start without a fright.
Touchdown! Says the announcer, as your boss says here's your promotion,
Now you can celebrate your hard work with joyful tears of emotion.

Rise
by Maya Bloom

In the darkness is when
We reach for the stars.
We realize how strong we are
When we climb up from our lowest valley.
Once we reach the summit,
Broken and bleeding,
Satisfaction is truly felt.
So rise and be all that you can be,
And stand proud,
For you have reached the next galaxy.

A Road of Hardship
by Steven Wilson

The wind is ever changing; its silent whisper rushes past my ears.
It speaks fear to my heart and death to my body, though my spirit strives on.
The road I travel is covered with thorns and thistles, and my feet run bare,
though my flow of love goes on.
Wild beasts may cross my path and try to destroy me,
though I will stay with faith and keep to God's commands.
My spirit will be humbled, my soul ever grateful
for the love of my Father in Heaven.
I have joy at peace and in pain and love for all people.
Riches I will not keep, self pride I will not wear, and sin I will not hold.
For I must follow in the footsteps of Christ.
The Kingdom of Heaven I will seek
and the Holy Spit will guide me through my troubles.
In my weakness, my spirit is strong and my work rewarding;
the truth I will proclaim from the rooftops
and though I be struck down, I will not fall, evil will not prevail over me.
Rough the path may be and sharp the swords of my enemies,
but I will hold firm and by my Lord I will stand.
Even unto death I am saved, I have full faith in my Lord Jesus Christ;
let the obstacle not overwhelm the runner
for all things are possible through God.
Forgiveness I will freely give, righteousness I will show,
and life I will restore with prayer.
Not a moment without suffering, and not a second without hope,
I go to fulfill the purpose God has given me.

Holiday Feelings
by Melanie Moore

A shining sign of light for all to see,
When one may stroll down the side of the street.
From outside I can see the Christmas tree.
It makes the Christmas spirit feel complete.
That old familiar scent of peppermint
Refreshes memories of winters past.
Though I am stuck in this nostalgic stint --
This spirit will, for a good while, still last.
I hear melodic sounds where're I go.
The music seems to rain down from the sky.
It often makes me wish for falling snow.
I hope this Christmas spirit will not die.
I reach my house, with the lights all aglow
And I decide to watch a Christmas show.

The Little Snowflake
by Jacob Goodman

What little burden snowflakes bear
flying freely through the air
never looking backwards, never looking forwards
no real goal that it points towards
from what we can see they are all the same
no differences at all, they have no name
so simple, no complexity to see with the eye
just something to come with cold, and with warmth to die
but when one looks deeper they begin to see
they are more than they were once made out to be
every one different in its own special way
it can shed a new light with so much to say
just an insignificant little snowflake falling to the ground
if one doesn't listen closely they'll never hear a sound
some dreams left unheeded because of the environment in which they fall
this phenomenon is purely by chance and strikes no fairness at all
how can one hope to make a difference when there are so many?
What it will do is unknown, but without one should there really be any?
These perfect little snowflakes moving throughout the day
each one's impact is there, even if they themselves have nothing to say.

My Lonely Heart
by Jessica Scordo

The way you ended things, broke my heart.
I knew deep down inside you were upset
To find out how you tore me apart.
But I can't figure out on how we met.
Either way, I really liked you.
We had a lot of fun when we were alone.
Even when our best friends were there too.
I miss spending time in your room at home.
I wonder how I'm going to fix my lonely heart.
This is really hard to get over you.
Seems how I drew you lots of romantic art
I never thought my heart would be in two.
On the day I told you "I was falling for you,"
You told me you didn't want a serious relationship.
Now I feel like crying every day,
Until the day I can get fixed, I'll be taking a trip.

Watching
by Sara Korb

I walk around with careful moves.
I watch my steps and their placements.
I'm being followed, I can sense it.
As my tracks disappear, yours replace them.
No matter what time of day, or the weather conditions,
My loneliness no longer exists as you invade it.
No matter which way I go or even how far I travel,
My steps are never clean and are never alone.
I can turn left, or even turn right.
But no matter where I turn I'm not out of sight.
You're sneaky and you're quiet,
You follow me around without great reasoning.
You know I know, and you still don't care.
You stare and grin, leaving me uncomfortable.
I can't be myself, or even act how I want.
You're the reason I can't seem to live a real life.
No matter how hard I ever try and swerve and go my own way,
You will always stay and keep me from moving on.
Is this how you want to spend your life?
Watching me have to worry about living mine?

Berries
by Christina Gee

Indigo balloons
are being tugged by the peddler
on their yellow-gold strings.
Children point
and ask their parents
for a penny
as they choose their own
special bit of blue joy.

Breath
by Alexandria Trombley

She stands, looking across the field:
across memories and time and nothing.
The smell of a crisp spring day fills her
as she gives into the land–
into the grass and the gravel
and the simplicity of it all.
The simplicity which moves her
Rather, floats her to a moment: a single beat of life–
a single life flashing before her in a beat–
A breath where sitting in the valley of grass,
the hands of wind fanned her auburn locks,
and the world was just still.

Forever Alone
by Elizabeth Drago

Why did your life have to come to an end?
So suddenly, without any warning.
You were all I had, you were my best friend
Now I spend my days all alone mourning.
Memories are all I have left of you.
I still hear your laughter as days pass by.
Not a day goes by that I don't feel blue.
I know your safe, but all I do is cry.
Is it too much to ask for one more day?
Just one more time to be with you. That's all.
One last hug so my life won't seem so grey
Losing you makes my world nothing but small.
So I guess this is goodbye forever.
My life will never be the same, not ever.

People
by Samantha Stevenson

I Don't Understand
Why people put others down
Why people think they're better
Than everyone else
Why they can't give others a chance
Why I'll never fit in because I don't
Look like you
What I really don't understand is
Why we change who we are to fit in
Why we are a different person at school than at home
Why we care what you think
Why your ways are always right
What I understand the most is
Why the ones who are themselves are happier
Why we smile for no reason
Why we have friends that are there for us no matter what
Why we don't get butterflies, we get a swarm
Why we don't give up
And that's why
We are who we are

I Believe
by Jillian Hecker

I believe in the power of music. A sweet lullaby that can sing you to sleep;
The confusing words of rap;
the beating of the drums that will take your soul on a journey
That selflessness and bravery aren't really that different
The ability to do anything you set your mind to
I believe in family; those who are always there and those who are never there
I believe in the things that we cannot see
Creatures like fairies, witches, dragons, and ghosts.
But, I don't believe what people say behind my back
I believe in looking someone in the face, and telling them what you really feel
I believe in the power of knowledge; its good and dark sides
I believe that a single choice can either
Destroy you, transform you, or change you, for better or for worse.
And I believe that one day,
The hatred that has had a hold on this world for centuries,
Will finally, one day, disappear.

Phoenix
by Anna Genes

A balloon full of air, potential energy, a sentence being said
All leading up to a reaction
Air forced out, kinetic energy, breathless speechlessness
All leading to deflation
A standstill moment
the wind in the sails gone dead
the body gone numb
All leading to the question
Now What?
Exhausted frustration sparks ideas
the flame ignited
From a standstill, filling with heat, filling with power
Zero to sixty, tangible triumph
Once again a full balloon
The kick to the finish, arms outstretched, rising from the ashes
Reaching up above
Grabbing hold of the stars that have just been born

Trapped In Your Subconscious
by Christain Horne

You open your eyes and its dull and grey. Your lost within your own subconscious.
You don't know how you get there or how you're going to escape.
You suddenly begin to feel alone and then you wonder if life was always like this.
You wonder if you are the reason you are here
or if this is some kind of strange dream.
You begin to cry. Realizing there is nothing left,
you submit yourself into the darkness of your subconscious.
Something is keeping you from going into the dark.
You open your eyes and it is still dull and grey.
In the distance you see a small light.
Something inside you tells you to go toward it.
As you get closer you see what appears to be the human form
of your subconscious.
You stare and then ask, are you what brought me here.
There's a flash and then you are brought back to reality.
Released from your subconscious.

The Heart
by Zoë Scoutt Loridas

is as beautiful,
and slow beating,
as a ballad
written for one's true love.
It's flowing words, flowing through,
red with emotions, are what keeps one alive.

Dreams of You In Heaven
by Willow Moulton

As I fall asleep and drift in and out of my heavy sleep,
I hear your voice, but it's as if I can't reach you.
I drift off a little more into the darkness.
I can feel myself relaxing and getting lighter but then I feel you coming closer.
I seize the moment and push myself into the darkness just a little closer.
Then I smell it, that scent that smells so familiar.
Closer, just a little closer. I can feel myself getting weaker.
My heart pounds and pounds but then you disappear
And everything's gone just like before.
I open my heavy eyes and turn to my side and look at your picture.
The last thing I have of you since God decided to take you.
I know you're here, and I know you're listening
But just wait for me up there, while I'm here.

Balance
by Isabella Agrusa

Calm view, my eyes open distinctly to the rich, blue hue
I ponder on the precious moments of my past
Wondering if regret is always a losing bet
Questioning each decision as if that moment was my last.
But is it wise to send all of my mistakes to the skies?
To push all unwanted emotions over the edge?
I watch the waves crash, seeing the calm sea and severe rocks mash
I now realize that with good comes bad as I gaze beyond the ledge.
I decide that I will vow to focus on the now
I will live in the present where happy and sad come and go
Finding balance is the key to living my life free
It's time to embrace everything in this world and go with the flow.

Him and I
by Teaganne Hoekstra

The touch of his hand on my face
the breath that he breathes on my face
His loving words, "It will be fine."
His calm eyes looking into mine
Holding him tight, holding me tight
Never wanting to say goodbye

The Look Out
by Sabrina Gregor

Here's to the skaters
And ice fishers too
Out under the cold wintry skies
It's all a true view
Cheers to the summertime
Where fast boats catch my eye
When I wish upon shooting stars
And when sailboats glide off into the night sky
Looking out into the distance
It's such a beautiful bay
This is where I live
And love to getaway

Farmyard
by Sarah McKinney

The strong smell of manure– yards
and yards of fences … Buildings here and there,
with animals and workers everywhere.
Horses in the pasture galloping, the pigs in the
pasture swimming in mud. Chickens eating feed
in their coupe, and cows chowing down grass in their
pasture. Goats needing petting while the sheep are huddling.
The farm is a busy, busy place.
The hay spread everywhere over the property, stepping
on it at almost every turn, the Barn at the top of the smaller
hill, with the farm house at the top of the larger hill, almost
over looking the whole property. A great sense of life, and
liberty on the farm.

Forgiven
by Morgan Parker

This tiny piece of paper could be my life– balled up and ripped into pieces; it's not.
It's a green leaf that feeds on the sun's shine.
Each of my cells help me grow bigger and bigger
even when the sun isn't effulgent.
I have been given the ability to breathe without water
and to fight with no hands.
I was given a second chance.
This tiny piece of paper could have been my life.

Everything Is Precious
by Gabrielle Homberg

Memories overflow the mind,
Watching them go down one by one.
A memory can never remain the same,
But rather feels like it weighs a ton.
Beauty is not hard to find.
It comes to shine by the sun.
A certain one can only claim
That the beauty has spun.
Life has a unique way to unwind.
One should cherish what has been done.
Everything has its own fame.
Then one can see how this life begun.

Start a New Life
by Diana Cai

It's winter in a new place
New people, new language, new land
Learning is a challenge
It's hard for me to understand
It's a Chinese New Year
A party is planned I fear
Will I be able to converse?
With guests from far and near
The night celebration is over
No problem meeting new friends
Language really doesn't separate
The warm feelings a party sends

Autumn Grass
by Kristina Lyons

Autumn grass is a brigade of soldiers
prepared for battle,
ready for whatever
this war might throw at them.
Understandably they are thirsty
from their days spent in the sun,
parched, in fact,
from the rigors of this campaign
See them there perspiring
as they stand in their camouflaged fatigues,
bravely facing this predicted defeat.

The Beauty of Nature
by Ananya Shah

In our World there are two Parts
One where the Beauty lies in Arts
The other in Nature
Has captured me
For it is a place with no Fees
Where magnificent trees are all one sees
Trees and Trees with stories untold
Branches on branches remain on hold
Yes, the World has two parts
But only One lies in my Heart

Watercolors
by Megan Tisdel

God is a weathered artist,
working alone in His tired studio.
Along one side, though,
are a row of windows,
so that the open sky surrounds Him.
As the sun peeks in,
He prepares his brushes,
the tubes of orange, red,
blue, and pink;
quietly a landscape is brought to life.
And with the dust that falls from the ceiling,
collecting on the painting,
clouds form.

Memories
by Gina Di Trapani

From the days he always smiled,
To the day he passed away,
I knew he'd always be with me
No matter the time of day.
With his pearly white teeth
And his top notch advice.
He truly was my hero
You don't have to ask me twice.
Papa you are my guardian angel
Always shining down on me
Even on the coldest days
You were with me, I could see.
Out of all my days, there's one I'll never forget
That horrendous day you went to heaven.
It's forever engraved in my memory.
November 5th, 2011.

The Other Half of Me
by Halimah Rosanally

When I was a kid, things were going pretty fast,
Didn't realize it would soon be the past.
Don't ever think for a moment
That your life can't change.
It's how much you matter to me that makes it worth the pain.
I've been thinking of you so much lately,
Now would be when I need you the most.
Nothing can change what was meant to be;
I didn't want to think about it, so I'll set it aside and move on.
Sometimes I feel like it's the end of the world,
Then I realize it's just for a while.
I do miss you and sometimes I feel left out
When I hear people talking
And never mentioning your name.
Is that the reason, why I hide inside?
Wanting to be normal,
Wishing I could change back time.
I'd have been grateful, though I was just a child.

The Praying House Spider
by Hannah Warren

Scittery-Scat, the little Spider descended down from her roost to pray,
Down to a corner she did glide to hear what God had for her to do
When, with a piercing light she was found out and fast did God's words wane,
As fast as her eight legs could carry her, she flew.
Thoughts of her mother, father, and aunt crept into her mind as she ran,
Silly of her to have ran at all really, with that obvious six pointed star on her back.
The footsteps were pounding, the chase was on now,
Her very nature against one man.
The chase is over,
And the little spider comes to terms with her world right before the smack!
Her funeral bed she has naught,
But a small dent of dust and there she will likely stay,
Poor little thing, hadn't she known she had no right to be
Only so much right as you or me.

I Wish
by Joise Smith

I wish to find that place,
the one with no hate,
the one with no jealousy.
I wish to find that place,
the one with no fear,
the one with no judgment.
I wish to find that place,
the one that's welcoming,
the one that's caring.
I wish to find that place,
the one that's loving,
the one that's kind.
With you I find that place,
the place that's pure and true,
the place that's whole and happy.
With you I find that place,
the place that's just right for you and me,
the place that's for the world to be.
I LOVE YOU

My Dearly Father
by Hope Geiger

I am sassy and sweet
I wonder if my dad can hear me
I can hear my father talking to me
I see a bright light like the sun in the sunlight
I want to go to Heaven to see my father
I am sassy and sweet
I pretend to see my dad walk down the Heaven's stairs
I feel my dad hugging me
I touch my father's heart
I worry about my father
I cried when I found out that he was dead
I am sassy and sweet
I understand that my father is dead
I say if you love someone you should let them go
I dream that he will be living with me again
I try to make him proud
I hope he will come back to live again
I am sassy and sweet

My Mind
by Chelsea Koschmider

My shadows are the footsteps I've walked and turned into flames.
What's left of me is the ashes of my remains.
Goosebumps rise on my flesh as my breath stutters while I gulp in the black air.
The burning in my mind makes me infuriated at the slightest touch.
Fire burns through my veins, bleeding me out and suffocating me.
My throat is as dry as a jumble of lies.
A lump clogging my stomach to let the hatred settle in me.
Bleeding tears exit my eyes in a thrown attempt to feel.
Death twisting around my body like a snake that coils around its frightened prey.
Having my last breath sucked out into a giant warp, freezing it above my head.
My ears turn cold like ice filling me with pure realization.
Fear makes my tongue feel swollen and thick with numbness.
I open my screaming eyes and lift my heavy head and look around.
It was all in my mind.

Flowered Wallpaper
by Anna Johnson

One day I found a closet empty as could be
Inside flower wrapped walls were all you could see,
When I was gazing at the petals I found a little tear,
I pinched it gently and tore the walls bear,
Skeletons dropped from the walls and stood and moved around,
They circled, looking me up and down,
As I ran for help a dozen hands pulled me back inside,
A voice whispered into my ear, "It's too late girl, now you're mine."

Perseverance
by Rebecca Harrity

The warm, summer breeze.
A glimmer of you.
The rustling of the trees.
A shimmer of you.
Your arms wrapped in mine.
A dance with you.
Our moment lost in time.
A chance with you.
No matter the pain through the years
Nor the myriad tears
No matter the adversity we find
Our hearts will forever be entwined.

The Beautiful
by Madison Overbey

She sells you a great picture,
Where you're more than just a fixture;
You can control yourself,
As you roll in your wealth.
Becoming a star,
Whoever you are.
Just like a dream,
But is it all a scheme?
Creating a lush life,
Without causing a strife;
In barely any time,
You're at your prime.
Though if it all is easy to achieve,
Why do so many grieve?

A Bat With a Broken Wing
by Jacob Bradley

A bat with a broken wing.
He could not see, nor hardly move.
Useless some say,
As they pass him off.
But had they seen what I have
They should never say again.
As he stumbled through the church door,
Sat in his seat, and slouched in sadness
He rubbed his eyes. A tear.
Lonely, helpless, afraid, he reached
For the only thing in which he comforted:
Faith. Would I be so strong?
No man is useless.
Nay, not even the bat with a broken wing.
Never again shall he be forgotten
Nor deserted.

Red Wings
by Clara Trippe

On the wall there is a picture
Of a mother holding her daughter,
Both with long red hair.
But in the living room
She lays in a plastic bed,
A woolen cap covering her purple scalp,
Eyes yellowed from the drugs.
I take the daughter away,
Past the grown-up's whispers
"A few more days"
To the swings.
Our legs dangle
Making us fly higher,
Catching our squeals in our throats.
Our fingers reaching to grab the sky.
The mother was in the doorway.
Looking
Not at me, but at the daughter
Watching her long red hair touch the sky
As if it were wings flying away.

War's Toll
by Lindsey Smith

His name is no longer Bill, John, or Hank,
the ground rumbles as he drives his tank.
Rat-a-tat-tat, he shoots his gun,
his name is no longer Chai, Ling, or Won.
His dog tags jingle
his blood does tingle
His name is no longer Gustav, Frank, or Miller,
Your son is now dubbed a killer.
Where did the boy go that you once knew,
a monster now lurks in his eyes oh so blue.
Tagged by the devil, he wears scars of sin,
a wolf hiding beneath a tattered sheep's skin.
In the name of his country he may kill dozens
shooting and killing brothers and cousins.
Killing and killing until he is slain
by others doing exactly the same.

Looking Up
by Gino Lombardo

Standing at the base looking up,
It feels as if I am out of luck.
As the time passes I can always wonder,
While I look at the peak up above yonder.
The first step to start my climb,
Will be the end to all my crime.
Grasping on ice with both my hands,
Realizing how high this mountain stands.
Midway on my journey I stumble down,
I get back up, but with a frown.
Finding myself back at square one,
I trace my steps, but this time I run.
Full of fatigue about to surrender,
My goal comes in mind and I become a contender.
When I finally meet this structure's peak,
I'll remember the times when I was weak.
No longer timid I will find my way,
Up to the top without a delay.
This mountain and I head to head,
Is a never ending journey I will no longer dread.

Six Marches
by Mariah Longacre

When
is such a lonely word
it fades at the end,
on the tip of your tongue
it's quiet, it lingers
as if sand through your fingers
so quiet
It waits in the air
the moment is spoken
plays finely tuned strings
to the hearts of the broken.

A Forgotten Promise
by Angela Tomas

As the wolf travels alone, through the dead, silent woods,
He hears a wail of a wolfess. She is lost, lonely, hungry, and freezing.
The wolf comes in contact with the wolfess and comforts her.
He goes searching the woods for hours until he finally finds a deer,
Chasing after it and killing it, to bring to the wolfess as his language of love,
Promising that they will be together forever.
The wolves have been living together in the woods for almost a year now.
They are in deep love.
But their new home feels vacant and as quiet as a church mouse.
The pair look at each other, smiling,
Knowing what they need to feel happy and stronger together.
Children. The wolf and wolfess bring forth children to the world!
Not one or two baby wolves, but three!
But one night, the wolf, searching for food, runs into a she-wolf.
He was stunned by her beauty!
She lured him away from his pack and didn't return home 3 days later.
When he arrived home, he was feeling dizzy,
His face was extremely red and his pupils dilated.
The wolfess and the little wolves were asleep
But awoke with a frightened look on their faces!
They were really scared of how the wolf was acting.
The wolf, with his horrifying, horrendous and hair-raising look,
Attacked the wolfess.
The little innocent wolves had a pale, ghost-like look on their faces.
They couldn't believe what they had seen. Tears shed from their ice-blue eyes.
He abandoned his loved ones for the wicked and evil.
The wolf forgot his promise and the wolfess and her little wolves forgot him.

Ode To My Piano
by Lauren Dessinger

You take away my greatest fears
And right the wrongs of many years.
When I was a child things were rough
And you taught me to be tough
Strength was then measured by precision.
Life, love, happiness have no division.
You allow me to hurt you.
Though I try not to.
I beat you out of tune
Until the keys are black and blue
You are the only one I can count on
Turn my sorrows into song.
When tears stream down my face
You make up for their mistakes.
You are no mere object to me
But God helping my soul to see
As long as I live, good things come and go
But lights will always bring me home.

Faded
by Barton L. Foster, Jr.

I wander these streets, aimlessly, as midnight draws near
while the stars weep bitter tears.
Pain in the very notion of breathing.
I walk through this cold wasteland as I stare into the dark abyss above.
My heart long since mangled, my smile long since forgotten.
My dreams have perished and my love was lost.
No remorse, without regret the world moves on,
time unhalted as if nothing's wrong.
I fall, scared and broken inside unable to hold back the pain any longer.
Time passes on, the scream of my soul doesn't cease
I begin to break under the pressure of the pain this tragedy has caused.
As I start to lose myself in the darkness,
silver rays cut through the black clouds showering me in light.
I peer into the night, voices beckoning me back to the surface of my mind.
I stand and look into my reflection on the ground and realize the pain-
stricken grimace that once occupied my expression was now a grin of hope.
Now I walk in stride towards home, the weight of grief lifted from my shoulders
and the chains of pain turned to relief all because of the voices so familiar
crying out not to give up, move on,
the voices of those who care, that won't let me fall, my friends.

Dawn of Darkness
by Paige Proper

Hunted in the dark,
Running from an unknown enemy.
Being stalked in a forest,
No way out.
Traveling in a circle,
Passing the same landmarks.
Growling in the distance,
Son of a wolf.
Human DNA and a wolf seed.
Werewolf.
Crawling through the dark,
On the forest floor.
This is the night of the werewolves,
Run for your life.
This is the night of the werewolves,
Never get out alive.
Tearing of flesh and cracking of bones,
Sounds of desperate screaming.

A Raven's Call
by Richard Dayson

Deep in the shadows, a castle stands abroad
Its stone walls are all but bare
Once a place of life, now falling in despair
Former decedents hanging on the wall
Bidding their time, waiting to fall
The ballroom cast an eerie glow
Putting the woods in a trance
High above the rafters, the moonlight its only light
When midnight strikes, the castle is stilled
The ghostly king watches over his kingdom in silence
In the darkest corner, a raven stands guard
A raven's call, summons the slumbering dragon
To ward the thieves and protect the jewels
In the chamber they glisten, in the dead of night
Watch where you step and take a deep breath
Dare to wake the castle, it will invite you in
For the call of the raven, will bring no haven

That Day
by Sabrina Senninger

For you have passed and gone, since the day you went with the dawn.
For you found your way, to the side of your wife that day.
In those coming days, in many different ways,
memories were remembered and shared, and your stories compared.
As many tears were shed, and heartfelt condolences said.
Family and friends came together again, to say goodbye and one last amen.
The angels came for you that day, to bring you on your way.
To an everlasting life, in Heaven with Christ and your wife.

That Day
by Addison Gale

The anger braided my body
It surged through my veins
It clenched my fists
It ruined my moment
I don't know what to do
I question my abilities
The crowd stood still
No one spoke
It was silent
It's ...
Not
Over
Yet

Twisted Hole
by Amy McCarty

Her bright blue, glass eyes
Push past your dark blue, frozen soul,
Capturing all memories in my head,
Bad or good, black or white.
Making a spider web
Of your twisted lies,
Grasping onto
The downward spiral of a life.
The wicked corn maze rustles at the bottom,
Sparkles towards the top,
Slowly crawling out
Of this crummy, black, twirling hole.

I'm Just Like You
by Amanda Thomas

Just because I'm overweight
Doesn't mean I don't have a heart
I have feelings too, don't you?
You should think about that sometime
Just because I'm overweight
Doesn't mean I don't eat healthy
But I like to splurge once in a while too, don't you?
Everyone likes to eat sweets
Just because I'm overweight
Doesn't mean I don't exercise
I like to jog, don't you?
We should go together sometime
Just because I'm overweight
Doesn't mean I'm not like everyone else
So please don't treat me differently

A Holocaust Memorial
by Shalenah Ivey

To children whose cries weren't comforted
To women whose tears weren't dried
To men whose life was anguished
To all who suffered and died
Your despair shall not be forgotten
Your memory not put aside
Your life will be resurrected
And your glory kept alive
In hearts you will remain
In conscious buried heavy
Dear people your faces engraved
Your perseverance will always amaze
May God never let us forget
Or may the savage history never fade
Your courageous souls of honor
Will always be a beacon
And this light never to weaken

Remember
by Stephanie Vickers

For one moment
Remember me
If only for one day
Remember me
Don't cry for me
Cry for us
Remember us?
Please remember me
For just one minute
Remember me
If you ever cry
Cry for us
Remember us?
I loved you
Don't ever forget me

Actors
by Hailey Stangebye

Let me take you on a Journey,
but I will warn you from the start:
I am not
Who I say I am– lies
"To be or not to be?"
"From sea to shining sea!"
I pop in for afternoon tea.
And sip, pinkie out
my index on the
Trigger– lies
Your screens and curtains bar me,
I peek inside for inspiration
but you are propped on your gurney.
lies from Lies
true lies from true Lies.
But, at least I am honest.

Reprieve
by Sierra Kudsin

It was a dark and rainy summer night.
He got a call that she could not be found.
He hoped she had not yet seen the white light.
The fear and anxiousness was all around.
He sat next to his brother, full of hope,
But when they found the note, their hearts both sank.
They opened his garage and they couldn't cope.
To find her, hanging, like she walked a plank.
My mother told me the news and I cried
For days. She was my aunt and my best friend.
I just could not believe that she had died.
I hope and I pray that his heart will mend.
Despite what she did, I will still believe,
She loves my family, and then, reprieve.

America
by Mercedes Kowalski

Once great and powerful
Hopeful, young, naïve
Always wanting more
Full of dreamers
Patriotism runs deep
In the land of the free
Through beautiful mountains
With majestic mountains
Crazy, stupid fun
Wild and free
Breaking barriers
Climbing ladders

Music
by Samantha Aviles

I have a riddle for thee
That I would like you to answer for me
What rises, falls, and swells
That captures men's souls as if by spells
It could bring people to tears in joyous rapture
Their hearts and souls it doth capture
Be it thunderous and loud or soft and sweet
Many the ear does it meet
This begins where words leave off
At its majestic splendor one cannot scoff
The more pleasure for you
If you've made a breakthrough
In solving this little riddle

Look Up
by Elizabeth Oderkirk

It's the same moon

No matter where you are
I know I can look up and see
the moon that you see too

Do you see me?

Though we are apart
Can you see me in
your mind's eye?

I can see you

I wish on the stars
Above that you were
with me. Holding me.

Seeing me.

But you're there, not
here.
Apart from me.

But we can always look up
because
It's the same moon.

Affected
by Elizabeth Delianites

Who knew cruelty could come in such a handsome package?
That twinkle in your eye seems so innocent,
You can make or break me with a quick glance.
You have such a sweet smile and a venomous tongue.
Your words cut through me like the sharpest knife that plunges right through me,
Twisting and turning, I shudder.
But I will stand tall,
Be reborn from the ashes like a phoenix,
Take this poison and spit it back at you,
I will never show my pain because I've seen worse and remained unbroken.
You may linger in my thoughts from time to time,
But it is brief and short lived for I've had enough,
I am now free from you and your fickle, indecisive ways,
Free to have control over my thoughts,
Free to be my own person,
Free to never again be affected by you like I was before.

My Generation
by Keenya Eason

These days, kids are so very different,
I swear we grew up so fast.
It is like yesterday, we were riding bikes and playing with toy guns
and now we're hiding and always having to run.
Brainwashed by the media–
trend-setters turn into bums,
wannabes into the people with success.
Congrats, hope one day I can be that blessed!
All the others are dead because what they were taught made sense,
but that brought them to an early deathbed.
We started with the following–
look how lollipops turned into blunts,
high fives turned into sex,
kisses turned into giving birth,
children into drug dealers.
Now what is a kid to do?
What has the media brought us to?
Laughs turn into rumors and puddles into blood baths.
Dreams turn to death,
and this is what my generation constantly goes through.

My Shoes
by Christine Meurer

My Ballet Shoes
My feet turn on the ground
But at the same time
I feel no pain, pointing
With that pink soft cloth
For out into the distances
It's a line that never ends
These ballet shoes are the story
Of my life for my whole life
Each mark and dent has a meaning
I will never let you go my best friend.

Be You
by Julia Langro

The world is filled with different kinds of people
Some may be cruel, some may be mean
Some may be nice, or somewhere in between
The spirit within someone is what makes them unique
A person can break a person
Though maybe not physically
Judgment can hurt a person critically
Be the person who thinks because hurtful words
can make the soul deteriorate helplessly
A person is a person and we all make mistakes
People often fill the shoes of bystanders
Not many stand up and act as a commander
Be an upstander because a person can be
permanently damaged by our ignorance
The best thing a person can do is offer a helping hand
The smallest act of kindness can cheer up someone's day
Sometimes a person is so conflicted,
that they're thinking their life will have to pay
Be the person to step up and save a life
Some people think that they aren't needed in the world;
that they're not wanted
Everyone is needed and everyone is wanted by someone that isn't that far
Just know that there is always going to be somebody
who loves you for just the way you are
Be the first to break away from the crowd;
to step up, stand up, and start a chain reaction

The Darkness
by Matthew Yearsley

Where did my true happiness go?
I seem to have misplaced it.
Life has suppressed and fought
And possibly erased it.
Why must life have trials?
Why did they target me?
I have traded youthful optimism
For negativity.
I spend my days drowning in my thoughts
Gasping desperately, searching for air.
I have my own demons
And my mind is their lair.
I look up at the clear, opaque sky
And see a solitary star, twinkling, it is.
I reach for it, and hope it is
My way out of The Darkness.

Trophy
by Julianna Zachowski

How long?
How long have I been sitting here?
How long have I watched the flames dance and crackle?
How long ago did I watch the skin blister and split, only to be devoured?
How long?
Why?
Why did I do it?
Why did I light the all-consuming inferno?
Why did I observe muscle char, flexing limbs as it tightens?
Why?
I answer myself,
One hundred and twenty minutes,
One for each year I was imprisoned.
I answer myself,
Because he was the one that put me there.
I tip my water on the fire, extinguishing the blaze.
I remove the now clean skull from the ashes,
I walk away with the trophy grasped tightly in my hand.

A and a
by Jessica Murphy

One A is broad and bold
Sweet and sensitive
Warm and wonderful
Caring and charming
The other a is kind and kindling
Evoking and exacerbating
Sardonic and sexy
Lovely and loud
One A is here and home
Indecisive and inherent
Pesky and placate
Honest and hellish
The other a is far and few
Annoying and aloof
Rude and revolutionizing
Godly and groundbreaking
One A is my new heart
the other a is where it was

Sinful Bliss
by Jocelyn Serrano

His pleasure is my pain,
Six feet under screams,
Yet no one can hear, my love, my fear;
For the dark creatures holding me here.
The bruises, the beating, the love and the pain,
His love and his brushes over and over again,
Like a nightmare with a blissful end,
The memories, the pain floods back to me all the same;
Like a lifetime before this little game.
Wanting and un-wanting for this to end,
His loving, his pain, to make amends;
For the times I was stupid to fall,
For the times I trusted and gave my all.
What I had; gone, most precious;
No longer there;
Lost viciously; Stolen without a care,
Now only I am forced to believe what isn't there,
And the only thing I have to say is that I loved the monster tenderly;
Without mercy.

Body Image
by Gabrielle Caputo

Every day she looks in the mirror
And can't help but frown
Her friends tell her she's beautiful
But she still stays down
They say "don't diet" and "you look fine"
But their words don't quiet the words in her head
Nothing seems to work, and the pounds stay on
She thinks maybe I'll lose more if I don't eat instead
Because even if it's an irrational fear
Her body weight is the cause of every tear
She has never cried over anything the way she cries over this
The mere sight of the number on the scale steals her bliss
For her happiness is only an illusion
And her smile simply a shield
She won't let anyone know the truth
The truth about how she really feels

The Process of Belief
by Stephen Skelly

In a welter of night,
Huddled masses clinging
To tattered flags for warmth;
Recycling the past for immediate need.
Through it all, we amble forth,
A persevering, grueling climb,
Our mountains engulfed in
Repentance and deceit.
Silence beckoned, releasing
Guttural roar. Wisdom collapsed,
Into full retreat. Honesty
And truth because wispy apparitions.
The twisted, torment,
Make-believe evolved
Into novel verity;
And we acquiesced.
The process of belief,
An elixir when weak;
A barren torpor of indecision;
We indulge on the sneak.

3rd
Place

Adriane Tharp

Man Overboard
by Adriane Tharp

Amelie was sealed inside herself like a Russian doll,
secrets written in the splinters of her wooden skin.
The people believed that if they shut out the sound,
it would cease to exist,
so eyes were averted from Amelie.
She cried diamonds into a satin pillowcase at dusk
while the moon retraced footprints in pursuit
of a mutual friend they used to know.
Beautiful and sad she scribbled in the sand with her finger.
She fell asleep on the shore to the waning echoes of Sea Foam Sound
and the ghostly awareness that his palm was still protected in hers.
The surf stole beautiful from the sands
and sad was all that remained of Amelie.

2nd Place

Emily Curtin

Appassionato
by Emily Curtin

Music enraptures this daughter of Eve
Emotion bursting from euphonious note
'tis built and dies with harmony
Mystery in tenuous stroke
Trebling or purely flat
Music proclaims in waves
Pathos, Eros, Lovers' spat
A ruthless villain's rage
In life, in love, in God, in trust
Our lives with music we must equate
Project meaning, our thoughts discussed
Yet with diminuendo its grandeur grows faint
Yes music enraptures this daughter of Eve
It overwhelms with a longing innate.

Mary Bertschi

One of the finest submissions of the year,
and perhaps our sentimental favorite,
belongs to Mary Bertschi.
Mary is a tenth grade student with immense talent.
The following example of her work
paints a wonderfully vivid picture of the passage of time.
Thank-you, Mary.

Silver Scars
by Mary Bertschi

What she remembers are little sausage fingers,
Galaxies of paint, and glitter, dancing across ivory palms.
Tiny hands grabbing and giving,
All with dirt under nubby nails.
Years etched themselves into
A child's hands with silver scars
And with each passing season, new lines.
Time flew by and nails grew,
And paint was replaced
By cherry varnish and filed tips,
And she continued to search for
The dirty grubby hands she knew.
New yet familiar hands
Illuminated from behind by the glow from car taillights,
And in the front glowing with light from the rising sun.
The last thing she remembers
Are those hands she grew up with,
And loved,
Trailing out a sad car window
And slowly waving goodbye.

Index
of
Authors

Index of Authors

Index of Authors

Index of Authors

Index of Authors

Discovered
Price List

Initial Copy 32.95

Additional Copies 24.00

Please Enclose $6 Shipping/Handling Each Order

Must specify book title and name of student author

Check or Money Order Payable to:

The America Library of Poetry
P.O. Box 978
Houlton, Maine 04730

Please Allow 4-6 Weeks For Delivery

THE AMERICA
LIBRARY OF POETRY

www.libraryofpoetry.com

Email: generalinquiries@libraryofpoetry.com

24